# Grammar Galaxy
## Mission Manual

Blue Star

Melanie Wilson, Ph.D.

GRAMMAR GALAXY Mission Manual: Blue Star
Copyright © 2020 by Fun to Learn Books

All rights reserved. This book may not be reproduced or transmitted in any form or by any means without written permission from the author.

ISBN: 978-1-7354939-1-6

# Table of Contents

Table of Contents ............................................................................................................ 1
A Note to Teachers ......................................................................................................... 4
A Note to Students .......................................................................................................... 5
Unit I: Adventures in Literature ...................................................................................... 6
    Mission 1: Literature Unit Study ................................................................................ 7
    Mission 1: Update ...................................................................................................... 13
    Mission 2: Tone & Mood ........................................................................................... 16
    Mission 2: Update ...................................................................................................... 23
    Mission 3: Short Stories ............................................................................................. 25
    Mission 3: Update ...................................................................................................... 33
    Mission 4: Allusions ................................................................................................... 35
    Mission 4: Update ...................................................................................................... 41
    Mission 5: Narrative Poems ....................................................................................... 43
    Mission 5: Update ...................................................................................................... 51
    Mission 6: Nonfiction Reading Comprehension ....................................................... 53
    Mission 6: Update ...................................................................................................... 63
    Mission 7: Urban Legends ......................................................................................... 65
    Mission 7: Update ...................................................................................................... 71
    Mission 8: Shakespeare ............................................................................................. 73
    Mission 8: Update ...................................................................................................... 81
    Mission 9: Satire ........................................................................................................ 83
    Mission 9: Update ...................................................................................................... 89
Literature Challenge 1 .................................................................................................... 91
Literature Challenge 2 .................................................................................................... 97
Unit II: Adventures in Spelling & Vocabulary ............................................................. 101
    Mission 10: Science Vocabulary ............................................................................. 102
    Mission 10: Update .................................................................................................. 111
    Mission 11: Oxymorons ........................................................................................... 115
    Mission 11: Update .................................................................................................. 121
    Mission 12: Onomatopoeia ...................................................................................... 123
    Mission 12: Update .................................................................................................. 131

- Mission 13: British vs. American English Spelling ............... 135
- Mission 13: Update ............... 143
- Mission 14: British Vocabulary ............... 145
- Mission 14: Update ............... 153
- Mission 15: Confused Vocabulary Words ............... 155
- Mission 15: Update ............... 163
- Mission 16: Vocabulary Mnemonics ............... 165
- Mission 16: Update ............... 173
- Mission 17: Prefixes, Suffixes, and Root Words ............... 177
- Mission 17: Update ............... 185
- Mission 18: Spelling High-Frequency Words ............... 187
- Mission 18: Update ............... 197

Spelling & Vocabulary Challenge 1 ............... 199
Spelling & Vocabulary Challenge 2 ............... 205

Unit III: Adventures in Grammar ............... 209
- Mission 19: Diagramming Sentences ............... 210
- Mission 19: Update ............... 219
- Mission 20: Grammatical Mood ............... 222
- Mission 20: Update ............... 229
- Mission 21: Infinitives ............... 231
- Mission 21: Update ............... 239
- Mission 22: Progressive Tense ............... 241
- Mission 22: Update ............... 249
- Mission 23: Adverbial Clauses & Phrases ............... 251
- Mission 23: Update ............... 259
- Mission 24: Relative Pronouns ............... 261
- Mission 24: Update ............... 269
- Mission 25: Misplaced Modifiers ............... 271
- Mission 25: Update ............... 279
- Mission 26: Dashes & Parentheses ............... 281
- Mission 26: Update ............... 289

Grammar Challenge 1 ............... 291
Grammar Challenge 2 ............... 297
Unit IV: Adventures in Composition & Speaking ............... 301

Mission 27: Parallel Structure .................................................................................. 302

Mission 27: Update ............................................................................................... 309

Mission 28: Morning Pages ................................................................................... 311

Mission 28: Update ............................................................................................... 317

Mission 29: Passive Voice ..................................................................................... 319

Mission 29: Update ............................................................................................... 327

Mission 30: Profile Essays .................................................................................... 329

Mission 30: Update ............................................................................................... 337

Mission 31: Writing Summaries ............................................................................ 339

Mission 31: Update ............................................................................................... 345

Mission 32: Persuasive Speaking .......................................................................... 347

Mission 32: Update ............................................................................................... 353

Mission 33: News Articles .................................................................................... 355

Mission 33: Update ............................................................................................... 361

Mission 34: Compare-and-Contrast Essays ........................................................... 363

Mission 34: Update ............................................................................................... 369

Mission 35: Slogans .............................................................................................. 371

Mission 35: Update ............................................................................................... 379

Mission 36: Gift Poems ........................................................................................ 381

Mission 36: Update ............................................................................................... 387

Blue Star Final Challenge 1 ...................................................................................... 389

Blue Star Final Challenge 2 ...................................................................................... 395

# A Note to Teachers

This isn't your average language arts workbook. In fact, it is a mission manual your guardian will use to save Grammar Galaxy from the evil Gremlin. In other words, it's supposed to be fun!

**You or your student should read a chapter in the *Grammar Galaxy Blue Star: Adventures in Language Arts* text first. If your student prefers to have you read the text, please do so.** Your student will then complete each step of the corresponding mission in this *Blue Star Mission Manual*. Provide as much help in reading and completing the missions as your student requires. The Activity section of each mission may require your assistance.

Each step of a mission may be completed on separate days or all at once, depending on interest level and schedule. Missions are short, so students stay motivated and have time to read and write in other ways they enjoy.

Students will be asked to use vocabulary words in a sentence verbally. Sample sentences are given. All vocabulary words are taken from the text. Vocabulary will improve with repeated exposure. Don't worry if your student doesn't recall word meanings. Exposure to the words is most important.

Missions marked "For Advanced Guardians Only" can be given to students who want to complete them as well as older students who are using Blue Star.

When all three steps of a mission are completed, you or your student should read the Update letter. Solutions to the missions are included with the update letter for students to check their own work. If you prefer to hide the solutions from your student, you may wish to fold the Update letter over and paper clip it with the solutions inside. You may also choose to remove the letter/solutions page from the book. A paper perforator can make the removal process neater. Some parents deliver the letter in an envelope to their student and even include stickers or another small treat. You can then review the solutions together. You may wish to hide the challenge solutions at the end of each unit in the same way. **For students who want more practice with a particular skill, be sure to check the website for resources at GrammarGalaxyBooks.com/BlueStar.**

Share your student's completed missions in the Grammar Guardians group on Facebook at Facebook.com/groups/GrammarGuardians or on Instagram and tag @GrammarGalaxyBooks. Your student has a chance to be chosen as Guardian of the Month and will receive Official Grammar Guardian mail.

To use *Grammar Galaxy* with more than one student, purchase a digital version of the mission manual with copying rights for your family or purchase additional printed mission manuals. Copying from the printed workbook is a violation of copyright. Thank you in advance for your integrity.

**Have a question?** Contact the author at grammargalaxybooks@gmail.com.

# A Note to Students

When you have read the story in the *Adventures in Language Arts* text, you are ready to complete the corresponding mission.

The first step of each mission includes review questions in the On Guard section. If you aren't sure of an answer, reread the text or your mission on that topic.

When you've completed all three steps in the mission, you'll receive an update letter from the royal English children that includes solutions for you to review.

Any time you need assistance, ask your teacher. With permission, you will find additional practice pages and activities at GrammarGalaxyBooks.com/BlueStar.

# Unit I: Adventures in Literature

## OFFICIAL GUARDIAN MAIL

**Mission 1: Literature Unit Study**

Dear fellow guardians of Grammar Galaxy,

The other kings in our universe are upset with our father. They believe he sent them a rude letter that was actually sent by the Gremlin.

Our mother has an idea to improve intergalactic relations: a literature unit study. If we get the young people of all galaxies working together, she hopes they'll forget all about the letter. We'll be doing a literature study of *Island of the Blue Dolphins*, but you may study any book you choose.

Father said to tell you that this mission is very important to the future of Grammar Galaxy. He thanks you in advance for your work.

Sincerely,

*Kirk, Luke, and Ellen English*
Guardians of Grammar Galaxy

☆ Step 1: On Guard and Choose a Book to Study

**On Guard.** Read each sentence. Use a highlighter to mark whether it is TRUE or FALSE.

1. A literature unit study may also be called a novel unit study.   TRUE   FALSE

2. A literature unit study is multi-subject learning based on a book or series of books.   TRUE   FALSE

3. Math is usually part of a literature unit study.   TRUE   FALSE

4. Science in a literature study may include studying the animals mentioned in a book.   TRUE   FALSE

5. Art in a literature study may include doing an author study.   TRUE   FALSE

**Say each of these words in a sentence.** *Examples are given.*

| **sanctimoniously** – self-righteously | "My bed is already made," my sister said **sanctimoniously**. |
|---|---|
| **narcissist** – self-centered person | My dad says the senator is a **narcissist** who only wants power. |
| **wryly** – humorously | "Your baby brother sure is messy," my friend observed **wryly**. |

**Choose a book to study.** Decide on a book to use for your literary unit study and write its title and author below.

Title for literary unit study_____

Author_____

The best books for unit studies incorporate many interesting subjects. You will find books and unit studies to consider at GrammarGalaxyBooks.com/BlueStar.

## ⭐ Step 2: Choose Topics to Study

*Brainstorm topics to study for each subject in the chart below. You may use a premade unit study for inspiration. Highlight at least one topic that you are most interested in for each subject (language arts, history, geography, science, art).*

|               | Vocabulary  | Theme      | Author     |
|---------------|-------------|------------|------------|
| **Language arts** |             |            |            |
|               | Time period | Music      | Games      |
| **History**   |             |            |            |
|               | Location    | Culture    | Food       |
| **Geography** |             |            |            |
|               | Animals     | Weather    | Technology |
| **Science**   |             |            |            |
|               | Scene       | Characters | Style      |
| **Art**       |             |            |            |

## ⭐ Step 3: Plan Unit Study Activities with Your Teacher

*For each topic you highlighted in Step 2, research activities with your teacher. Write what book you'll read, video you'll watch, or project you'll create for each. Add any supplies you need. You may plan activities using a digital organizer instead. Begin reading your book and working on these unit study activities. Put an X in the Complete column for each activity you finish.* **Note:** <u>You do not have to complete all the activities before moving on to story and Mission 2.</u>

| Topic | Activity | Supplies | Complete |
|---|---|---|---|
| | | | |
| | | | |
| | | | |
| | | | |
| | | | |
| | | | |
| | | | |
| | | | |
| | | | |
| | | | |
| | | | |
| | | | |
| | | | |
| | | | |
| | | | |
| | | | |
| | | | |
| | | | |
| | | | |
| | | | |
| | | | |

**Vocabulary Victory!** *What do each of these words mean? Check Step 1 if you need a reminder.*

| sanctimoniously | "Your father sent a rude letter and now he is paying the price for it," she said **sanctimoniously**. |
|---|---|
| narcissist | They believe I'm a power-hungry **narcissist**. |
| wryly | "That usually means a lot of work for us," Luke said **wryly**. |


☆ Advanced Guardians Only

**Create a 9-week plan for completing your literary unit study on the next page.** *Divide the number of your book's chapters by 9. The answer is the number of chapters you will read each week, leaving the remainder of the chapters for the last week.* <u>Island of the Blue Dolphins</u> *has 29 chapters, and 29 divided by 9 is 3 with 5 left over. We will read chapters 1-3 in Week 1, chapters 4-6 in Week 2, and chapters 25-29 in Week 9.*

When you have your reading plan down, you'll plan 2-3 activities to complete that week. If you want to match the activities to the reading, you'll need to skim the chapters to see what topics are introduced.

Your finished plan could be used by other students in the universe!

Unit Study for Book Title_____

| Week | Chapters | Activity 1 | Activity 2 | Activity 3 |
|---|---|---|---|---|
| 1 | | | | |
| 2 | | | | |
| 3 | | | | |
| 4 | | | | |
| 5 | | | | |
| 6 | | | | |
| 7 | | | | |
| 8 | | | | |
| 9 | | | | |

# OFFICIAL GUARDIAN MAIL

**Mission 1: Update**

Dear fellow guardians,

Our mother's plan worked! In fact, several kings in the universe have contacted Father to congratulate him on bringing the students of the universe together.

We have been having a marvelous time with our *Island of the Blue Dolphins* unit study. We've learned so much from the other galaxies. We know you have, too. We love the unit studies you've put together! In fact, when we finish *Island*, we're going to start another book study. Maybe you'd like to join us?

Sincerely,

*Kirk, Luke, and Ellen English*
Guardians of Grammar Galaxy

P.S. This is a good time to have you sign the Guardian of the Galaxy Pledge for the year. You'll find it following the solutions to the On Guard section. You're ready to read Chapter 2 in the Adventures book.

Mission 1: Literature Unit Study

Step 1 Solutions
**On Guard**.
1. A literature unit study may also be called a novel unit study.                TRUE   FALSE
2. A literature unit study is multi-subject learning based on a book or series of books.   TRUE   FALSE
3. Math is usually part of a literature unit study.                              TRUE   FALSE
4. Science in a literature study may include studying the animals mentioned in a book.  TRUE   FALSE
5. Art in a literature study may include doing an author study.                  TRUE   FALSE

# Guardian of the Galaxy Pledge

I am committed to fulfilling my duties as a guardian of Grammar Galaxy, the most important of which is to read. I pledge to choose good books that I can read myself or have read to me. I will do my very best to read every day so I can learn, enjoy life, and keep the galaxy strong.

Signed,

_____

Date:_____

## OFFICIAL GUARDIAN MAIL

**Mission 2: Tone & Mood**

Dear guardian friends,

Have you been in a bad mood or have you been disrespectful? We recently learned that bleak and sarcastic were the mood and tone of the month on planet Composition. Most likely this was the Gremlin's doing.

We are thankful our mother canceled the Mood and Tone of the Month program. But we realized we all need to understand mood and tone in literature. We are including information from *The Guide to Grammar Galaxy* that you'll need to complete this mission.

Sincerely,

*Kirk, Luke, and Ellen English*
Guardians of Grammar Galaxy

P.S. Keep working on your literature unit study.

## Tone & Mood in Literature

Tone and mood can help the reader understand the theme or main idea of a literary work.

**Tone is the author's attitude toward the characters, events, and audience.** Tone is determined by the vocabulary used and the syntax or arrangement of words. Tone may be described as serious, lighthearted, sarcastic, depressed, humorous, wary, and more. Edward Lear's "There Was an Old Man Who Supposed" has a mocking, teasing tone.

There was an Old Man who supposed,
That the street door was partially closed;
But some very large rats ate his coats and his hats,
While that futile [pointless] old gentleman dozed.

**Mood is the feeling or atmosphere of a piece of literature that is most notable at its beginning.** The setting, illustrations, and vocabulary are used to create mood. Mood may be romantic, mournful, cheerful, hopeless, optimistic, playful, etc. The beginning lines of "Drowned at Sea" by Henry Kendall create a dark, depressing mood.

Gloomy cliffs, so worn and wasted with the washing of the waves,
Are ye [you] not like giant tombstones round those lonely ocean graves?

Mission 2: Tone & Mood

## ⭐ Step 1: Stay On Guard & Identify Mood

**On Guard.** *Read the sentence. Use a highlighter to mark TRUE or FALSE for each.*

1. An author study can be part of a literature unit study.    TRUE   FALSE

2. A study of theme can be part of a literature unit study.    TRUE   FALSE

3. Mood is most notable at the end of a book.    TRUE   FALSE

4. Tone is a reader's attitude toward a book.    TRUE   FALSE

5. Mood and tone can help a reader identify the theme.    TRUE   FALSE

**Say each of these words in a sentence.** *Examples are given.*

| | |
|---|---|
| **sanctions** – punishment | Grounding is the most common form of **sanctions** at my house. |
| **infraction** – offense | The **infraction** my mother won't tolerate is disrespect. |
| **indifference** – unconcern | My older dog shows **indifference** when our puppy nips at her. |

Mission 2: Tone & Mood

**Identify mood.** *For each picture below, highlight the most likely mood.* **Hint**: <u>Look up any words you don't know in a dictionary</u>.

1. peaceful      eerie      playful

2. romantic      pessimistic      playful

3. mournful      humorous      hopeless

4. romantic      humorous      sad

5. mournful      playful      pessimistic

6. adventurous      mournful      eerie

7. serious      optimistic      romantic

Mission 2: Tone & Mood

## ⭐ Step 2: Identify Tone
**Read each sentence and highlight its most likely tone.** *Note:* <u>Look up the meaning of any words you do not know.</u>

1. Cook said, "I don't know what came over me, Your Highness!"
indignant            conciliatory         lighthearted

2. The queen hugged her friend with tears in her eyes.
warm                 irascible            hopeless

3. "I was in such a mood that my cat thought I had lost my mind!"
serious              inspirational        playful

4. The queen explained what had happened on planet Composition.
serious              inspirational        playful

5. When the queen answered Cook and told her what she'd said, Cook covered her face with her hands.
eerie                mournful             optimistic

6. The queen hugged Cook again and told her all was well.
lighthearted         playful              optimistic

7. After the queen told her what the king had said, Cook chuckled, "If I'd been thinking straight, I would have refused to give him dessert!"
humorous             morose               cantankerous

8. "I'm ready to get back to the castle—my happiest place on earth," Cook said.
indifferent          warm                 sarcastic

**Activity.** Find and begin reading a book that has your desired mood. The cover, description, and first pages will give you clues to the book's mood.

Mission 2: Tone & Mood

## ⭐ Step 3: Rewrite Sentences in a New Tone

**Read the quotes.** *Rewrite them so that they are in the new tone indicated in parentheses. Keep the quotation marks, but you may change the wording and add description after the quote. An example is given.* **Note:** <u>Look up the meaning of any words you don't know.</u>

"You're not the boss of me." (playful)
"You're not the boss of me, you stinker," Ellen said, tickling the preschool boy.

1. "I said I'm not the maid." (subservient)
___
___

2. "Mother, I'm fine." (enthusiastic)
___
___

3. "Yes, I agree with you." (fearful)
___
___

4. "I'm saying it's all hopeless." (optimistic)
___
___

5. "Where are you off to?" (suspicious)
___
___

6. "I haven't had a day off in ages." (wistful)
___
___

7. "Is it okay with you if I take one?" (playful)
___
___

8. "It's okay that you take a day off." (sarcastic)
___
___

Mission 2: Tone & Mood

**Vocabulary Victory!** Do you remember what these words mean? *Check Step 1 if you need a reminder.*

| sanctions | You deserve serious **sanctions**. |
|---|---|
| infraction | You deserve serious sanctions for this **infraction**. |
| indifference | Ellen's **indifference** worried her. |

☆ Advanced Guardians Only
**Rewrite the following paragraph in a lighthearted mood using your own words.** The paragraph from "East of the Sun and West of the Moon" by Peter Christen Asbjornsen has a dark, eerie mood. Change the setting and description so that something tapping on the windowpane feels playful.

So one day, 'twas on a Thursday evening late at the fall of the year, the weather was so wild and rough outside, and it was so cruelly dark, and rain fell and wind blew, till the walls of the cottage shook again. There they all sat round the fire, busy with this thing and that. But just then, all at once something gave three taps on the windowpane.

_____
_____
_____
_____
_____
_____
_____
_____
_____
_____
_____
_____
_____
_____
_____
_____
_____
_____

**Mission 2: Update**

Dear guardians,

You did a great job with mood and tone in this mission. I (Ellen) am particularly happy that you changed the mood of the paragraph from "East of the Sun and West of Moon." It was giving me the creeps!

Our mother wanted us to remind you that guardians should avoid using a sarcastic tone with parents and others in authority.

We are including the solutions to your mission.

Sincerely,

*Kirk, Luke, and Ellen English*
Guardians of Grammar Galaxy

P.S. We are grateful for your help!

Mission 2: Tone & Mood

Step 1 Solutions

**On Guard.**

1. An author study can be part of a literature unit study.  **TRUE**  FALSE

2. A study of theme can be part of a literature unit study.  **TRUE**  FALSE

3. Mood is most notable at the end of a book.  TRUE  **FALSE**

4. Tone is a reader's attitude toward a book.  TRUE  **FALSE**

5. Mood and tone can help a reader identify the theme.  **TRUE**  FALSE

**Identify mood.**

1. peaceful          **eerie**         playful
2. **romantic**      pessimistic       playful
3. mournful          **humorous**      hopeless
4. romantic          humorous          **sad**
5. mournful          **playful**       pessimistic
6. **adventurous**   mournful          eerie
7. serious           **optimistic**    romantic

Step 2 Solutions

1. Cook said, "I don't know what came over me, Your Highness!"
indignant     **conciliatory**     lighthearted
2. The queen hugged her friend with tears in her eyes.
**warm**          irascible           hopeless
3. "I was in such a mood that my cat thought I had lost my mind!"
serious         inspirational        **playful**
4. The queen explained what had happened on planet Composition.
**serious**      inspirational       playful
5. When the queen answered Cook and told her what she'd said, Cook covered her face with her hands.
eerie           **mournful**         optimistic
6. The queen hugged Cook again and told her all was well.
lighthearted    playful             **optimistic**
7. After the queen told her what the king had said, Cook chuckled, "If I'd been thinking straight, I would have refused to give him dessert!"
**humorous**     morose              cantankerous
8. "I'm ready to get back to the castle—my happiest place on earth," Cook said.
indifferent     **warm**             sarcastic

Step 3 Solutions – answers will vary

1. **"I said I'm not the maid." (subservient)** – "I'll be the maid because I made the mess."
2. **"Mother, I'm fine." (enthusiastic)** – "Mother, I feel fine," he said, smiling.
3. **"Yes, I agree with you." (fearful)** – "I'd like to agree with you," she said nervously.
4. **"I'm saying it's all hopeless." (optimistic)** – "I'm saying everything will be all right," he said with a smile.
5. **"Where are you off to?" (suspicious)** – "Where did you say you are off to?" she asked, eyes narrowed.
6. **"I haven't had a day off in ages." (wistful)** – "I haven't had a day off in ages," she said, eyes shining.
7. **"Is it okay with you if I take one?" (playful)** – "Is it okay if I take one, or will you miss me too much?" she asked
8. **"It's okay that you take a day off." (sarcastic)** – "Why wouldn't it be okay that you take yet another day off," she said, groaning.

**Advanced Guardians.** So it was a sunny morning in spring, after a light mist had watered the flowers until they sparkled like gem stones. There they sat around the breakfast table chatting, when they heard a friendly rap on the windowpane.

# OFFICIAL GUARDIAN MAIL

**Mission 3: Short Stories**

Dear fellow guardians,

Have you noticed that your books seem shorter? The Short Story Statute is to blame. The idea was to make novels shorter to help with shorter attention spans. The problem is that adapted novels don't always make good short stories. We need your help to tell the difference between shortened novels and true short stories. We are including information from *The Guide to Grammar Galaxy* to help you.

Our mother had the idea of having a Short Story Spotlight and reading short stories for this mission. We think it will be fun!

Sincerely,

*Kirk, Luke, and Ellen English*
Guardians of Grammar Galaxy

## Short Stories

A short story is prose fiction that can be read in one sitting. There are no firm guidelines for length, but typically short stories have word counts from 1,000-4,000 words. They are often organized into collections to create a full-length book.

In short stories, less time is spent developing the plot (problem/solution) and more time is spent developing a particular mood (emotion). These stories may not easily be categorized into a particular genre.

Short stories have a long history, beginning in oral storytelling, folk tales, legends, and myths. But they gained new popularity in the 1800s. Some famous short stories include "The Gift of the Magi" by O. Henry, "Rip Van Winkle" by Washington Irving, and "The Tell-Tale Heart" by Edgar Allen Poe.

**Novellas** are longer than short stories, having up to 40,000 words. Some novellas are full-length novels that have been adapted for children.

Mission 3: Short Stories

⭐ Step 1: Stay On Guard & Identify Short Stories
**On Guard.** *Use a highlighter to mark TRUE or FALSE for each statement.*

1. Mood and tone are the same.                                            TRUE     FALSE

2. <u>It was so cruelly dark</u> helps set the mood.                      TRUE     FALSE

3. The tone of "I'm happy to help" said with a warm smile is sarcastic.   TRUE     FALSE

4. A literature study is the same as a unit study of a novel.             TRUE     FALSE

5. "The Tell-Tale Heart" is a short story.                                TRUE     FALSE


**Say each of these words in a sentence.** *Examples are given.*

| | |
|---|---|
| **jauntily** – cheerfully | "When is it time for cake?" the boys asked **jauntily**. |
| **gratifying** – rewarding | My aunt says teaching is very **gratifying**. |
| **absent-mindedly** – distracted | My dog went through training **absent-mindedly**; he kept looking at the other dogs. |

Mission 3: Short Stories

**Identify short stories.** *Highlight whether each piece of literature described below is a short story, novella, or novel.* **Hint:** <u>Use the information from the guidebook to help you.</u>

1. "How the Camel Got His Hump" by Rudyard Kipling – in the collection *Just So Stories*.

short story          novella          novel

2. *A Christmas Carol* by Charles Dickens – 27,405 words

short story          novella          novel

3. *The Lightning Thief* by Rick Riordan – 87,290 words

short story          novella          novel

4. *Roll of Thunder, Hear My Cry* by Mildred D. Taylor – 73,660 words

short story          novella          novel

5. *Esperanza Rising* by Pam Muñoz Ryan – 40,890

short story          novella          novel

6. *The Little Prince* by Antoine de Saint-Exupéry – 17,255 words

short story          novella          novel

7. *Sherlock Holmes Retold for Children* by Mark Williams

short story          novella          novel

8. "The Golden Windows" by Laura E. Richards – in the collection *The Pig Brother and Other Fables and Stories*

short story          novella          novel

⭐ Step 2: Read "Thank You, M'am" by Langston Hughes

**Find websites for reading "Thank You, M'am" at GrammarGalaxyBooks.com/ BlueStar.** Then highlight the correct answers to the questions below.

**1. What is the setting of the story?**

store                    field                    night

**2. Which character seems fearful at the beginning of the story?**

Mrs. Jones               Roger                    neither

**3. Why does Mrs. Jones think Roger tried to steal her purse?**

hunger                   a dare                   buy shoes

**4. What did Roger do when Mrs. Jones said he could have asked her for shoes?**

ran                      dried his face           asked her why

**5. What does Mrs. Jones suggest about her past?**

she had plenty           she was in jail          she stole

**6. What <u>doesn't</u> Roger want when Mrs. Jones makes him something to eat?**

to be mistrusted         cocoa                    to be seen

**7. What does Mrs. Jones mean by "shoes come devilish like that will burn your feet"?**

the shoes won't last     he will get blisters     theft leads to punishment

**8. What is a main theme of this short story?**

theft                    kindness                 hard work

**Activity.** *Talk about what you would have done in Mrs. Jones's position and why.*

⭐ Step 3: Read "Rip Van Winkle" by Washington Irving

**Read or listen to any version of the short story "Rip Van Winkle."** See GrammarGalaxyBooks.com/BlueStar for options. Then answer the questions. Note that the story is set before and after the American Revolutionary War.

1. How would you describe Rip Van Winkle at the beginning of the story?

2. How would you describe Dame Van Winkle at the beginning of the story?

3. In the rising action, Rip takes his dog and gun and climbs a mountain. Why?

4. What changes have taken place while Rip was sleeping?

5. Is Rip more of an active (makes things happen) or passive (lets things happen) character? Give an example to support your opinion.

6. One of the themes of the story is freedom. What two types of freedom does Rip have after he wakes up?

7. What do you think the author's attitude is toward Rip? Give an example to support your opinion.

8. If Rip had it to do over again, do you think he would have taken the drinks that made him sleep for 20 years? Why or why not?

**Vocabulary Victory!** Do you remember what these words mean? *Check Step 1 if you need a reminder.*

| jauntily | "What books have you chosen?" he asked them **jauntily**. |
|---|---|
| gratifying | Reading is so **gratifying**. |
| absent-mindedly | The queen nodded **absent-mindedly**. |

 Advanced Guardians Only

**Write your own short story based on "Thank You, M'am" or "Rip Van Winkle."**
*Either write about an incident of unlikely kindness or write a short story about what happens when someone is gone for a long time and returns. Make notes in the table below before writing your first draft. Type or write your first draft outside of your mission manual.*

| Characters | Setting | Rising Action | Climax | Falling Action |
|---|---|---|---|---|
| | | | | |

## OFFICIAL GUARDIAN MAIL

**Mission 3: Update**

Dear guardians,

With your help, we have sent the short-story versions of novels to planet Recycling. But we are loving the real short stories we've been reading for Short Story Spotlight. We hope you have, too. If you love short stories, you can find a list of more to read at GrammarGalaxyBooks.com/BlueStar.

We have included the solutions to your mission.

Sincerely,

*Kirk, Luke, and Ellen English*
Guardians of Grammar Galaxy

Mission 3: Short Stories

Step 1 Solutions
**On Guard.**

1. Mood and tone are the same. — TRUE **FALSE**
2. <u>It was so cruelly dark</u> helps set the mood. — **TRUE** FALSE
3. The tone of "I'm happy to help" said with a warm smile is sarcastic. — TRUE **FALSE**
4. A literature study is the same as a unit study of a novel. — TRUE **FALSE**
5. "The Tell-Tale Heart" is a short story. — **TRUE** FALSE

**Identify short stories.**

1. "How the Camel Got His Hump" by Rudyard Kipling – in the collection *Just So Stories*.
**short story** | novella | novel
2. *A Christmas Carol* by Charles Dickens – 27,405 words
short story | **novella** | novel
3. *The Lightning Thief* by Rick Riordan – 87,290 words
short story | novella | **novel**
4. *Roll of Thunder, Hear My Cry* by Mildred D. Taylor – 73,660 words
short story | novella | **novel**
5. *Esperanza Rising* by Pam Muñoz Ryan – 40,890
short story | novella | **novel** – *but novella is acceptable*
6. *The Little Prince* by Antoine de Saint-Exupéry – 17,255 words
short story | **novella** | novel
7. *Sherlock Holmes Retold for Children* by Mark Williams
short story | **novella** | novel – *adapted novels are novellas*
8. "The Golden Windows" by Laura E. Richards – in the collection *The Pig Brother and Other Fables and Stories*
**short story** | novella | novel

Step 2 Solutions

1. What is the setting of the story?
store | field | **night**
2. Which character seems fearful at the beginning of the story?
Mrs. Jones | **Roger** | neither
3. Why does Mrs. Jones think Roger tried to steal her purse?
**hunger** | a dare | buy shoes
4. What did Roger do when Mrs. Jones said he could have asked her for shoes?
ran | **dried his face** | asked her why
5. What does Mrs. Jones suggest about her past?
she had plenty | she was in jail | **she stole**
6. What <u>doesn't</u> Roger want when Mrs. Jones makes him something to eat?
**to be mistrusted** | cocoa | to be seen
7. What does Mrs. Jones mean by "shoes come devilish like that will burn your feet"?
the shoes won't last | he will get blisters | **theft leads to punishment**
8. What is a main theme of this short story?
theft | **kindness** | hard work

Step 3 Solutions – answers will vary

**1. How would you describe Rip Van Winkle at the beginning of the story?**
good-natured, hen-pecked (criticized by his wife), beloved by children and dogs, lazy
**2. How would you describe Dame Van Winkle at the beginning of the story?**
critical, angry
**3. In the rising action, Rip takes his dog and gun and climbs a mountain. Why?**
To get away from farm work and his wife's criticism
**4. What changes have taken place while Rip was sleeping?**
His gun was rusted; he saw people he didn't know, dressed in an unfamiliar fashion; his beard was a foot long; his house was in decay; no one recognized him; his town was no longer under the king's rule
**5. Is Rip more of an active (makes things happen) or passive (lets things happen) character? Give an example to support your opinion.**
Passive. "His companion now emptied the contents of the keg into large flagons, and made signs to him to wait upon the company. He obeyed with fear and trembling…"
**6. One of the themes of the story is freedom. What two types of freedom does Rip have after he wakes up?**
Freedom from his critical wife and freedom from England's rule.
**7. What do you think the author's attitude is toward Rip? Give an example to support your opinion.**
Amused acceptance of his nature. "Having nothing to do at home, and being arrived at that happy age when a man can be idle with impunity, he took his place once more on the bench at the inn-door, and was reverenced as one of the patriarchs of the village…"

**Mission 4: Allusions**

Dear guardian friends,

As you may know, some members of Parliament want allusions removed from books, movies, and more to encourage understanding on our planet. But we think there is a better way. We can use an allusion that we don't know as motivation to learn.

In this mission, you'll be asked to identify allusions and determine what they mean. We are also asking you to write Parliament, urging them to reconsider an anti-allusion act. Thank you in advance!

May the force be with you,

*Kirk, Luke, and Ellen English*
Guardians of Grammar Galaxy

## ⭐ Step 1: Stay On Guard & Identify Allusion

**On Guard.** *Highlight TRUE or FALSE for each statement.*

1. "The Tell-Tale Heart" is a famous novella. — TRUE  FALSE

2. Short stories only recently became popular. — TRUE  FALSE

3. Mood is the author's attitude toward characters, events, and audience. — TRUE  FALSE

4. Mood is likely to be established at the beginning of a piece of literature. — TRUE  FALSE

5. Listening to music may be part of a literature unit study. — TRUE  FALSE

**Say each of these words in a sentence.** *Examples are given.*

| **engaged** – involved | Mom often uses games to get us **engaged** in doing chores. |
|---|---|
| **ruminating** – pondering | My sister keeps **ruminating** about her missing candy. |
| **cultural** – social | Our education includes attending **cultural** events. |

Mission 4: Allusions

**Identify allusion.** *Read each sentence. Then highlight whether the underlined portion is an allusion or a reference.* **Hint:** *Allusions are indirect.*

1. Luke likes to say, "I'll be back" like the robot character in *Terminator*.

    allusion             reference

2. When we are on a walk, Ellen likes to say, "Follow the yellow brick road!"

    allusion             reference

3. Our mother likes to say, "Ask not what your mother can do for you; ask what you can do for your mother."

    allusion             reference

4. When Luke was little, he kept repeating "I like them Sam I Am" from Dr. Seuss's *Green Eggs and Ham*.

    allusion             reference

5. After seeing *Frozen*, Ellen wouldn't stop saying "Let it go!"

    allusion             reference

6. Before Luke gets up to bat, he repeats, "I think I can, I think I can."

    allusion             reference

7. Mr. Wordagi likes to quote, "To thine ownself be true."

    allusion             reference

8. Sometimes Cook calls us poppet.

    allusion             reference

Mission 4: Allusions

⭐ Step 2: Research the Allusion

**Read the sentence.** *With your teacher's help and permission, research the source of the underlined allusion and write it under the sentence. You can find websites with the sources at GrammarGalaxyBooks.com/BlueStar.*

1. "One of these things is not like the others," Ellen joked.

2. "I'm strong to the finish 'cause I eats me spinach," Luke said proudly.

3. Luke pretends that he is Comet and says, "Be vewy vewy quiet. I'm hunting wabbits!"

4. Luke ran in and grabbed the cookie in front of Kirk, saying, "Meep! Meep!" as he left.

5. When the king saw Luke eating a new vegetable dish, he said, "He likes it! Hey, Mikey!"

6. "Remember the Alamo!" the king cried as he attacked Luke's position in the video game.

7. As the king urged his wife onto the zipline platform, he said, "The only thing we have to fear is fear itself."

8. At bedtime the queen likes to say, "I love you right up to the moon—and back."

**Activity.** *See if you can use an allusion that your teacher doesn't know.*

Mission 4: Allusions

⭐ Step 3: Write the Meaning of the Allusion

**Read the sentence.** *If you don't know the reference of the underlined allusion, see the websites listed at GrammarGalaxyBooks.com/BlueStar. Then write the allusion's meaning in the sentence using the space below.*

1. At bedtime when the children were little, the queen used to say, "Let the wild rumpus start!"

2. After a long trip with the family, the queen fell into bed saying, "There's no place like home."

3. When Kirk was having trouble with his schoolwork, the queen encouraged him to "just keep swimming."

4. Ellen was feeling blue, so the queen said, "Think of the happiest things. It's the same as having wings!"

5. The king says that long putts in golf are his Achilles's heel.

6. The children believe that Mr. Wordagi is a Jekyll and Hyde with his assignments.

7. The queen reminds her husband not to be a Scrooge at Christmas time.

8. The spaceball team's comeback has been called a Cinderella story.


**Vocabulary Victory!** Do you remember what these words mean? *Check Step 1 if you need a reminder.*

| engaged | It **engaged** the country in World War II. |
|---|---|
| ruminating | The king began **ruminating** aloud. |
| cultural | It keeps people with fewer **cultural** experiences from being left out. |

Mission 4: Allusions

☆ Advanced Guardians Only
**Write a positive letter to Parliament about allusions.** *Include the allusion "highly illogical" from Star Trek. Be sure to sign the letter.*

Dear Members of Parliament,
_____
_____
_____
_____
_____
_____
_____
_____
_____
_____
_____
_____
_____
_____
_____
_____

Live long and prosper,

_____

## OFFICIAL GUARDIAN MAIL

**Mission 4: Update**

Dear guardians,

You gave all her all she's got, Captain! That's an allusion from *Star Trek* to say that you gave your best effort to the mission.

The prime minister contacted our father and said that your letters convinced Parliament to stop pursuing the anti-allusion act. We can set phasers to stun. In other words, we don't have to keep fighting the act. But we must remain vigilant!

Keep researching allusions and using them in your writing. And remember: Do. Or do not. There is no try.

Be sure to check the solutions that accompany this letter.

Sincerely,

*Kirk, Luke, and Ellen English*
Guardians of Grammar Galaxy

Mission 4: Allusions

Step 1 Solutions

**On Guard.**

**Identify allusion.**

1. "The Tell-Tale Heart" is a famous novella.  TRUE  **FALSE**
2. Short stories only recently became popular.  TRUE  **FALSE**
3. Mood is the author's attitude toward characters, events, and audience.  TRUE  **FALSE**
4. Mood is likely to be established at the beginning of a piece of literature.  **TRUE**  FALSE
5. Listening to music may be part of a literature unit study.  **TRUE**  FALSE

1. Luke likes to say, "I'll be back" like the robot character in *Terminator*.
   allusion      **reference**
2. When we are on a walk, Ellen likes to say, "Follow the yellow brick road!"
   **allusion**      reference
3. Our mother likes to say, "Ask not what your mother can do for you; ask what you can do for your mother."
   **allusion**      referenc
4. When Luke was little, he kept repeating "I like them Sam I Am" from Dr. Seuss's *Green Eggs and Ham*.
   allusion      **reference**
5. After seeing *Frozen*, Ellen wouldn't stop saying "Let it go!
   allusion      **reference**
6. Before Luke gets up to bat, he repeats, "I think I can, I think I can."
   **allusion**      reference
7. Mr. Wordagi likes to quote, "To thine ownself be true."
   **allusion**      reference
8. Sometimes Cook calls us poppet.
   **allusion**      reference

Step 2 Solutions

1. "One of these things is not like the others," Ellen joked.
Sesame Street game
2. "I'm strong to the finish 'cause I eats me spinach," Luke said proudly.
Popeye cartoon
3. Luke pretends that he is Comet and says, "Be vewy vewy quiet. I'm hunting wabbits!"
Elmer Fudd in Bugs Bunny cartoons
4. Luke ran in and grabbed the cookie in front of Kirk, saying, "Meep! Meep!" as he left.
Road Runner from Looney Tunes
5. When the king saw Luke eating a new vegetable dish, he said, "He likes it! Hey, Mikey!"
Life cereal commercial
6. "Remember the Alamo!" the king cried as he attacked Luke's position in the video game.
1836 battle in the Texas revolution
7. As the king urged his wife onto the zipline platform, he said, "The only thing we have to fear is fear itself."
From President Franklin Delano Roosevelt's First Inaugural Address
8. At bedtime the queen likes to say, "I love you right up to the moon—and back."
From *Guess How Much I Love You* by Sam McBratney or the book *I Love You to the Moon and Back*

Step 3 Solutions

1. At bedtime when the children were little, the queen used to say, "Let the wild rumpus start!"
The kids will be loud and active (From *Where the Wild Things Are* by Maurice Sendak)
2. After a long trip with the family, the queen fell into bed saying, "There's no place like home."
While trips are wonderful, being at home is a relief. (from the book and movie *The Wizard of Oz*)
3. When Kirk was having trouble with his schoolwork, the queen encouraged him to "just keep swimming."
Keep going, even when it's hard. (from the movie *Finding Nemo*)
4. Ellen was feeling blue, so the queen said, "Think of the happiest things. It's the same as having wings!"
Positive thinking lifts our spirits. (from the movie Peter Pan)
5. The king says that long putts in golf are his Achilles's heel.
His weakness (from the Greek legend about Achilles who was killed by being struck in the heel—his weakest part)
6. The children believe that Mr. Wordagi is a Jekyll and Hyde with his assignments.
Has a personality that wavers between good and evil (from *The Strange Case of Dr. Jekyll and Mr. Hyde* by Lee Jeong-ju and Robert Louis Stevenson)
7. The queen reminds her husband not to be a Scrooge at Christmas time.
Selfish and greedy (from *A Christmas Carol* by Charles Dickens)
8. The spaceball team's comeback has been called a Cinderella story.
Losers-turned-victors (from the fairy tale)

**Mission 5: Narrative Poems**

Dear guardians,

You may have noticed that something was wrong at the Poetry Reading Festival. We weren't reading our poems with the right rhythm. There is a new poetry conductor—probably a Gremlin accomplice—who is emphasizing the wrong words and syllables. While our father has him dismissed, we need your help in determining the correct rhythm for rhyming poetry.

We each chose a narrative poem to read at the festival. Narrative poems are stories. We thought you would enjoy reading our poems for this mission. Kirk recommended that we not read his, however, to save time.

Thank you for completing this mission that will make next year's Poetry Reading Festival a lot more enjoyable.

Sincerely,

*Kirk, Luke, and Ellen English*
Guardians of Grammar Galaxy

Mission 5: Narrative Poems

## ⭐ Step 1: On Guard & Identify Emphasized Syllables

**On Guard.** *Answer the following five questions or answer them for your teacher verbally.*

1. What is a literature unit study?

2. What is used to create mood in literature?

3. A short story is prose fiction that can be read ____ _____ _____.

4. What is an allusion?

5. How is an allusion different from a reference?

**Say each of these words in a sentence.** *Examples are given.*

| **quipped** – joked | He didn't laugh when she **quipped** about his fear of spiders. |
|---|---|
| **halfhearted** – unenthusiastic | We gave the boring speaker **halfhearted** applause. |
| **pall** – gloom | A **pall** of sorrow filled the room when they said he was gone. |

Mission 5: Narrative Poems

**Identify emphasized syllables.** *Highlight the syllables that should be stressed or emphasized in <u>the second and third stanzas only</u>. The first stanza is done for you. Then highlight the answers to the questions that follow the poem.*
**Hint:** <u>Clap as you read</u>. *If you aren't sure where a syllable break in a word is, look it up in a dictionary.*

      Casey at the Bat
      Ernest Lawrence Thayer


The **out**look wasn't **bril**liant for the **Mud**ville nine that **day**:
The **score** stood four to **two**, with but one **in**ning more to **play**,
And **then** when Cooney **died** at first, and **Bar**rows did the **same**,
A **pall**-like silence **fell** upon the **pa**trons of the **game**.

A straggling few got up to go in deep despair. The rest
Clung to the hope which springs eternal in the human breast;
They thought, "If only Casey could but get a whack at that—
We'd put up even money now, with Casey at the bat."

But Flynn preceded Casey, as did also Jimmy Blake,
And the former was a hoodoo, while the latter was a cake;
So upon that stricken multitude grim melancholy sat,
For there seemed but little chance of Casey getting to the bat.

But Flynn let drive a single, to the wonderment of all,
And Blake, the much despised, tore the cover off the ball;
And when the dust had lifted, and men saw what had occurred,
There was Jimmy safe at second and Flynn a-hugging third.

Then from five thousand throats and more there rose a lusty yell;
It rumbled through the valley, it rattled in the dell;
It pounded on the mountain and recoiled upon the flat,
For Casey, mighty Casey, was advancing to the bat.

There was ease in Casey's manner as he stepped into his place;
There was pride in Casey's bearing and a smile lit Casey's face.
And when, responding to the cheers, he lightly doffed his hat,
No stranger in the crowd could doubt 'twas Casey at the bat.

Ten thousand eyes were on him as he rubbed his hands with dirt;
Five thousand tongues applauded when he wiped them on his shirt;
Then while the writhing pitcher ground the ball into his hip,
Defiance flashed in Casey's eye, a sneer curled Casey's lip.

45

And now the leather-covered sphere came hurtling through the air,
And Casey stood a-watching it in haughty grandeur there.
Close by the sturdy batsman the ball unheeded sped—
"That ain't my style," said Casey. "Strike one!" the umpire said.

From the benches, black with people, there went up a muffled roar,
Like the beating of the storm-waves on a stern and distant shore;
"Kill him! Kill the umpire!" shouted someone on the stand;
And it's likely they'd have killed him had not Casey raised his hand.

With a smile of Christian charity great Casey's visage shone;
He stilled the rising tumult; he bade the game go on;
He signaled to the pitcher, and once more the dun sphere flew;
But Casey still ignored it and the umpire said, "Strike two!"

"Fraud!" cried the maddened thousands, and echo answered "Fraud!"
But one scornful look from Casey and the audience was awed.
They saw his face grow stern and cold, they saw his muscles strain,
And they knew that Casey wouldn't let that ball go by again.

The sneer is gone from Casey's lip, his teeth are clenched in hate,
He pounds with cruel violence his bat upon the plate;
And now the pitcher holds the ball, and now he lets it go,
And now the air is shattered by the force of Casey's blow.

Oh, somewhere in this favoured land the sun is shining bright,
The band is playing somewhere, and somewhere hearts are light;
And somewhere men are laughing, and somewhere children shout,
But there is no joy in Mudville—mighty Casey has struck out.

1. **Is "Casey at the Bat" written in couplets or triplets?**

    couplets          triplets

2. **What is the tone of the poem?**

    mocking          serious

3. **What is the theme of the poem?**

    crowds          pride

Mission 5: Narrative Poems

## ⭐ Step 2: Identify the Ballad's Tone
**Read these lyrics to "April Showers" by Louis Silvers and B. G. Desylva.**
*Then answer the questions that follow the poem.*

Life is not a highway strewn with flowers
Still it holds a goodly share of bliss
When the sun gives way to April showers
Here is the point you should never miss

Though April showers may come your way
They bring the flowers that bloom in May
So if it's raining have no regrets
Because it isn't raining rain you know, it's raining violets
And where you see clouds upon the hills
You soon will see crowds of daffodils
So keep on looking for a blue bird
And list'ning for his song
Whenever April showers come along

And where you see clouds upon the hills
You soon will see crowds of daffodils
So keep on looking for a blue bird
And list'ning for his song
Whenever April showers come along

1. **Try to clap the rhythm of the poem. Is it easier or more difficult to find the rhythm of this ballad than for "Casey at the Bat"?**
   easier         more difficult

2. **What is the tone of the ballad?**
   bleak          encouraging

3. **What is the theme of the ballad?**
   patience       nature

**Activity.** *Listen to the song "April Showers." See GrammarGalaxyBooks.com/BlueStar for a website. Do you prefer the poem or the song?*

## ⭐ Step 3: Read "Annabel Lee" by Edgar Allan Poe
**Read the poem aloud with correct emphasis.** *Answer the questions that follow.* **Note:** *The word winged should be pronounced with two syllables to maintain rhythm.*

It was many and many a year ago,
   In a kingdom by the sea,
That a maiden there lived whom you may know
   By the name of Annabel Lee;
And this maiden she lived with no other thought
   Than to love and be loved by me.

*I* was a child and *she* was a child,
   In this kingdom by the sea,
But we loved with a love that was more than love—
   I and my Annabel Lee—
With a love that the wingèd seraphs of Heaven
   Coveted her and me.

And this was the reason that, long ago,
   In this kingdom by the sea,
A wind blew out of a cloud, chilling
   My beautiful Annabel Lee;
So that her highborn kinsmen came
   And bore her away from me,
To shut her up in a sepulchre
   In this kingdom by the sea.

The angels, not half so happy in Heaven,
   Went envying her and me—
Yes!—that was the reason (as all men know,
   In this kingdom by the sea)
That the wind came out of the cloud by night,
   Chilling and killing my Annabel Lee.

But our love it was stronger by far than the love
   Of those who were older than we—
   Of many far wiser than we—
And neither the angels in Heaven above
   Nor the demons down under the sea
Can ever dissever my soul from the soul
   Of the beautiful Annabel Lee;

For the moon never beams, without bringing me dreams
   Of the beautiful Annabel Lee;

Mission 5: Narrative Poems

> And the stars never rise, but I feel the bright eyes
>    Of the beautiful Annabel Lee;
> And so, all the night-tide, I lie down by the side
>    Of my darling—my darling—my life and my bride,
>      In her sepulchre there by the sea—
>      In her tomb by the sounding sea.

1. Look up the meanings of the words below and write short definitions.

   coveted –           seraphs –
   sepulchre –         dissever –
   kinsmen –

2. What is the mood of the poem? What words create the mood?

3. Why does the narrator believe the wind was sent to kill Annabel Lee?

4. What is the theme of the poem?

5. What do you think of how the narrator is managing his grief?

**Vocabulary Victory!** Do you remember what these words mean? *Check Step 1 if you need a reminder.*

| quipped | "By the time I've heard the children's practice readings, I could give them all by memory," the queen **quipped**. |
|---|---|
| halfhearted | The crowd gave **halfhearted** applause. |
| pall | A **pall**-like silence fell upon the patrons of the game. |

Mission 5: Narrative Poems

⭐ Advanced Guardians Only
**Write your own narrative poem.** *First, choose a brief plot for the story. Then write pairs of rhyming words you could use to tell the story and establish the mood and tone you want. Use a print or online rhyming dictionary for help. Next, write one couplet with the rhythm you'll be using. Finally, keep writing or typing the poem in a notebook or on a computer until you have a finished narrative poem. Read it out loud to make sure you have the rhythm right.*

Plot

_____

_____

_____

_____

Rhyming word pairs

|   |   |   |   |   |   |
|---|---|---|---|---|---|
|   |   |   |   |   |   |
|   |   |   |   |   |   |
|   |   |   |   |   |   |
|   |   |   |   |   |   |
|   |   |   |   |   |   |

Couplet

_____

_____

_____

**OFFICIAL GUARDIAN MAIL**

**Mission 5: Update**

Dear guardian friends,

Thank you for helping us read these poems with the right rhythm. We are relieved that Father has found a new poetry conductor. That will make the Poetry Reading Festival a lot better next year.

We think narrative poems are fun, and we hope you do, too. I (Ellen) liked the song version of "April Showers" so much that I'm going to learn to play it on the ukulele!

We are including the solutions to your mission.

Sincerely,

*Kirk, Luke, and Ellen English*
Guardians of Grammar Galaxy

P.S. Are you still working on your literature unit study?

Mission 5: Narrative Poems

Step 1 Solutions
**On Guard.**
1. What is a literature unit study?
**Multi-subject learning based on a book or series of books**
2. What is used to create mood in literature?
**The setting, illustrations, and vocabulary**
3. A short story is prose fiction that can be read ____ _____ _____.
**In one sitting**
4. What is an allusion?
**A figure of speech that indirectly refers to books, movies, people, or events.**
5. How is an allusion different from a reference?
**Allusions are indirect; references are direct and name the source.**

**Identify emphasized syllables.**

A straggling few got up to go in deep despair. The rest
Clung to the hope which springs eternal in the human breast;
They thought, "If only Casey could but get a whack at that—
We'd put up even money now, with Casey at the bat."

But Flynn preceded Casey, as did also Jimmy Blake,
And the former was a hoodoo, while the latter was a cake;
So upon that stricken multitude grim melancholy sat,
For there seemed but little chance of Casey getting to the bat.

1. **Is "Casey at the Bat" written in couplets or triplets?**
   couplets                 triplets
2. **What is the tone of the poem?**
   mocking               serious
3. **What is the theme of the poem?**
   crowds                pride

Step 2 Solutions
1. **Try to clap the rhythm of the poem. Is it easier or more difficult to find the rhythm of this ballad than for "Casey at the Bat"?**
   easier                  more difficult
2. **What is the tone of the ballad?**
   bleak                  encouraging
3. **What is the theme of the ballad?**
   patience               nature

Step 3 Solutions – answers will vary
1. **Look up the meanings of the words below and write short definitions.**

   coveted – wanted       seraphs – angels
   sepulchre – tomb       dissever – divide
   kinsmen – relatives

2. **What is the mood of the poem? What words create the mood?**
   Dark, depressing. Cloud, wind, night, chilling, killing, demons, etc.
3. **Why does the narrator believe the wind was sent to kill Annabel Lee?**
   Angels envied her and the narrator
4. **What is the theme of the poem?**
   Grief, lost love
5. **What do you think of how the narrator is managing his grief?**
   The narrator is depressed and not thinking clearly

**Mission 6: Nonfiction Reading Comprehension**

Greetings, guardians!

If your reading comprehension scores for the Galactic Aptitude Test have been low, you're not alone! We weren't doing well on our practice tests, and our mother discovered why. We weren't making connections to the reading passages so that they seemed important to our lives.

If you complete this mission, your nonfiction reading comprehension will improve and so will your GAT scores. Our father tells us that better comprehension means better grades in school and the ability to learn any subject we're interested in. We're ready to take on this challenge, and we hope you are, too.

Best wishes,

*Kirk, Luke, and Ellen English*
Guardians of Grammar Galaxy

## ⭐ Step 1: On Guard & Scan Nonfiction Article
**On Guard.** *Highlight a, b, or c as the best answer.*

1. A <u>ballad</u> is best described as a/an:
   a. allusion
   b. short story
   c. narrative poem

2. "Like Neil Armstrong, this is one small step for man, one giant leap for mankind" is a/an:
   a. reference
   b. allusion
   c. narrative poem

3. "The Tell-Tale Heart" by Edgar Allen Poe is a famous:
   a. short story
   b. ballad
   c. neither a nor b

4. The tone of "Casey at the Bat" is:
   a. bleak
   b. mocking
   c. wary

5. The mood of "Annabel Lee" is:
   a. lighthearted
   b. depressing
   c. mocking


**Say each of these words in a sentence.** *Examples are given.*

| **dismal** – depressing | The rainy forecast for our picnic was **dismal**. |
|---|---|
| **comprehend** – understand | Our dog doesn't **comprehend** our command to stop digging. |
| **primes** – prepares | The first layer of paint on the wall **primes** it for the new color. |

Mission 6: Nonfiction Reading Comprehension

**Scan nonfiction article.** *Read the first two paragraphs. Read the first two paragraphs in the excerpt of the article "Nanotechnology Facts for Kids" from <u>Kiddle Encyclopedia</u> below. Then look at the subtitles (in bold text) and images. Finally, highlight the best answer to the questions that follow.* **Note**: *<u>[sic] means that an error in the text is recognized but is printed uncorrected from the original source.</u>*

**Nanotechnology** is a part of science and technology about the control of matter on the atomic and molecular scale - this means things that are about 100 nanometres or smaller.

Nanotechnology includes making products that use parts this small, such as electronic devices, catalysts, sensors, etc. To give you an idea of how small that is, there are more nanometres in an inch than there are inches in 400 miles.

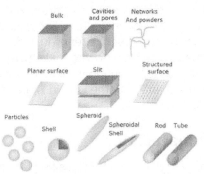

Typical nanostructure geometries.

To give a [sic] international idea of how small that is, there are as many nanometres in a centimetre, as there are centimetres in 100 kilometres.

Nanotechnology brings together scientists and engineers from many different subjects, such as applied physics, materials science, interface and colloid science, device physics, chemistry, supramolecular chemistry (which refers to the area of chemistry that focuses on the non-covalent bonding interactions of molecules), self-replicating machines and robotics, chemical engineering, mechanical engineering, biology, biological engineering, and electrical engineering.

Generally, when people talk about nanotechnology, they mean structures of the size 100 nanometers or smaller. There are one million nanometers in a millimeter. Nanotechnology tries to make materials or machines of that size.

People are doing many different types of work in the field of nanotechnology. Most current work looks at making nanoparticles (particles with nanometer size) that have special properties, such as the way they scatter light, absorb X-rays, transport electrical currents or heat, etc. At the more "science fiction" end of the field are attempts to make small copies of bigger machines or really new ideas for structures that make themselves. New materials are possible with nano size structures. It is even possible to work with single atoms.

There has been a lot of discussion about the future of nanotechnology and its dangers. Nanotechnology may be able to invent new materials and instruments which would be very useful, such as in medicine, computers, and making clean electricity (nanoelectromechanical systems) is helping design the next generation of solar panels, and efficient low-energy lighting. On the other hand, nanotechnology is new and there could be unknown problems. For example if the materials are bad for people's health or for nature. They may have a bad effect on the economy or even big natural systems like the Earth itself. Some groups argue that there should be rules about the use of nanotechnology.

## The start of nanotechnology

Ideas of nanotechnology were first used in talk "There's Plenty of Room at the Bottom", a talk given by the scientist Richard Feynman at an American Physical Society meeting at Caltech on December 29, 1959. Feynman described a way to move individual atoms to build smaller instruments and operate at that scale. Properties such as surface tension and Van der walls force would become very important.

Feynman's simple idea seemed possible. The word "nanotechnology" was explained by Tokyo Science University Professor Norio Taniguchi in a 1974 paper. He said that nanotechnology was the work of changing materials by one atom or by one molecule. In the 1980s this idea was studied by Dr. K. Eric Drexler, who spoke and wrote about the importance of nano-scale events. "Engines of Creation: The Coming Era of Nanotechnology" (1986) is thought to be the first book on nanotechnology. Nanotechnology and Nano science started with two key developments: the start of cluster science and the invention of the scanning tunneling microscope (STM). Soon afterwards, new molecules with carbon were discovered - first fullerenes in 1986 and carbon nanotubes a few years later. In another development, people studied how to make semiconductor nano crystals. Many metal oxide nanoparticles are now used as quantum dots (nanoparticles where the behaviour of single electrons becomes important). In 2000, the United States National Nanotechnology Initiative began to develop science in this field.

## Classification of Nano materials

Nanotechnology has nanomaterials which can be classified into one, two and three dimensions [sic] nanoparticles. This classification is based upon different properties it holds such as scattering of light, absorbing x rays, transport electric current or heat. Nanotechnology has multidisciplinary character affecting multiple traditional technologies and different scientific disciplines. New materials which can be scaled even at atomic size can be manufactured.

## Facts

- One nanometer (nm) is $10^{-9}$ or 0.000,000,001 meter.

- When two carbon atoms join together to make a molecule the distance between them is in the range of 0.12-0.15 nm.

- DNA double helix is about 2 nm from one side to the other. It develops into a new field of DNA nanotechnology. In future DNA can be manipulated that can lead to new revolution. Human genome can be manipulated according to requirements.

- A nanometer and a meter can be understood as the same size-difference as between [sic] golf ball and the Earth.

- One nanometer is about one twenty-five-thousandth the diameter of a human hair.

- Fingernails grow one nanometer per second.

## Physical characteristics of nanomaterial

At nano scale physical properties of system [sic] or particles substantially change. Physical properties such as quantum size effects where electrons move different for very small sizes of particle. Properties such as mechanical, electrical and optical changes when macroscopic system changes to microscopic one which is of utmost importance.

Nano materials and particles can act as catalyst [sic] to increase the reaction rate along with [sic] that produce better yield as compared to other catalyst. [sic] Some of the most interesting properties when particle gets converted to nano scale are substances which usually stop light become transparent (copper); it becomes possible to burn some materials (aluminum); solids turn into liquids at room temperature (gold); insulators become conductors (silicon). A material such as gold, which does not react with other chemicals at normal scales, can be a powerful chemical catalyst at nanoscales. These special properties which we can only see at the nano scale are one of the most interesting things about nanotechnology.

## Images for kids

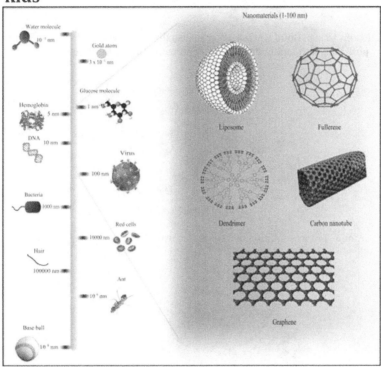

Comparison of Nanomaterials Sizes

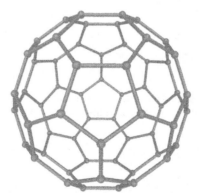

Buckminsterfullerene C60, also known as the buckyball, is a representative member of the carbon structures known as fullerenes. Members of the fullerene family are a major subject of research falling under the nanotechnology umbrella.

Image of reconstruction on a clean Gold(100) surface, as visualized using scanning tunneling microscopy. The positions of the individual atoms composing the surface are visible.

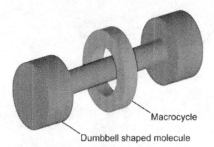

Graphical representation of a rotaxane, useful as a molecular switch.

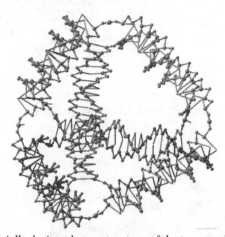

This DNA tetrahedron is an artificially designed nanostructure of the type made in the field of DNA nanotechnology. Each edge of the tetrahedron is a 20 base pair DNA double helix, and each vertex is a three-arm junction.

1. **The article is primarily about:**
   a. small matter
   b. technology for kids' toys
   c. geometry

2. **One of the subtitles in the article is:**
   a. physical characteristics of nanomaterial
   b. applications of nanomaterial
   c. buckyballs

3. **Nanostructures pictured do not include:**
   a. triangles
   b. rods
   c. particles

4. **Nanomaterials are smaller than:**
   a. hair
   b. bacteria
   c. both a & b

5. **The image of rotaxane is shaped like a:**
   a. buckyball
   b. dumbbell
   c. cube

Mission 6: Nonfiction Reading Comprehension

⭐ Step 2: Make Connections to Nonfiction Material
**Read each quote from the article "Nanotechnology Facts for Kids" given below.** *Then answer the questions.*

1. "Nanotechnology brings together scientists and engineers from many different subjects." Which of the subjects listed in the article is of most interest to you personally?

_____

2. "At the more 'science fiction' end of the field are attempts to make small copies of bigger machines…" What small copy of a big machine would you most like to have?

_____

3. "There has been a lot of discussion about the future of nanotechnology and its dangers." Are you more concerned with the benefits or the dangers of nanotechnology mentioned in the article?

_____

4. "Nanotechnology and Nano science started with two key developments: the start of cluster science and the invention of the scanning tunneling microscope (STM)." What have you examined under a microscope?

_____

5. "Fingernails grow one nanometer per second." Does it seem like your nails grow slower or faster than this?

_____

**Activity.** *Watch a video on nanotechnology. You'll find some listed at GrammarGalaxyBooks.com/BlueStar. Discuss what is most exciting about nanotechnology to you.*

Mission 6: Nonfiction Reading Comprehension

☆ Step 3: Read to Comprehend

**Read the "Nanotechnology for Kids" article excerpt from Step 1.** *Then answer the questions below. You may refer to the article to help you choose the best answer.*

1. **Nanotechnology tries to make materials or machines that are:**
   a. one million nanometers or larger
   b. 0.000,000,001 meter or smaller
   c. 100 nanometers or smaller

2. **Most current nanotechnology work is focused on:**
   a. nanoparticles with special properties
   b. surface tension
   c. DNA

3. **When used as catalysts, nanoparticles and materials:**
   a. produce better yields
   b. increase reaction rates
   c. both a and b

4. **With nanoparticles, it is possible for:**
   a. matter to disappear
   b. copper to become transparent
   c. gold to liquefy at temps below freezing

5. **According to the article, one of the most interesting things about nanotechnology is:**
   a. how small nanoparticles are
   b. the buckyball shape of fullerenes
   c. special properties we only see at nano scale

**Vocabulary Victory!** Do you remember what these words mean? *Check Step 1 if you need a reminder.*

| dismal | If kids don't understand what they're reading, the future is **dismal**. |
|---|---|
| comprehend | She knew they had the ability to read and **comprehend** well. |
| primes | Preparing to read nonfiction in this way **primes** your mind to make connections. |

Mission 6: Nonfiction Reading Comprehension

⭐ Advanced Guardians Only
**Read a nonfiction article on ancient Egyptian agriculture.** *See GrammarGalaxyBooks.com/BlueStar for an online option. Then complete the steps below.*

1. Read the title and a short section of text. Scan the images and subtitles. Write two subtitles below.




2. What knowledge or experience do you have of ancient Egypt?




3. What knowledge or experience do you have of agriculture/farming?




4. Read the article. Without doing further research, what similarities do you see between ancient Egyptian agriculture and modern agriculture?



5. Briefly describe ancient Egyptian agriculture based on the article you read.

**Mission 6: Update**

Dear guardians,

Our reading comprehension scores are going up! We are sure yours are, too. You did an excellent job on this mission.

The queen wants us to remind you to keep using these steps of scanning and making connections with nonfiction text before you read. She says your comprehension will keep improving.

We are including the solutions to this mission.

Sincerely,

*Kirk, Luke, and Ellen English*
Guardians of Grammar Galaxy

Mission 6: Nonfiction Reading Comprehension

Step 1 Solutions
On Guard.
1. A ballad is best described as a/an:
a. allusion
b. short story
c. narrative poem
2. "Like Neil Armstrong, this is one small step for man, one giant leap for mankind" is a/an:
a. reference
b. allusion
c. narrative poem
3. "The Tell-Tale Heart" by Edgar Allen Poe is a famous:
a. short story
b. ballad
c. neither a nor b
4. The tone of "Casey at the Bat" is:
a. bleak
b. mocking
c. wary
5. The mood of "Annabel Lee" is:
a. lighthearted
b. depressing
c. mocking

Scan nonfiction article.
1. The article is primarily about:
   a. small matter
   b. technology for kids' toys
   c. geometry
2. One of the subtitles in the article is:
   a. physical characteristics of nanomaterial
   b. applications of nanomaterial
   c. buckyballs
3. Nanostructures pictured do not include:
   a. triangles
   b. rods
   c. particles
4. Nanomaterials are smaller than:
   a. hair
   b. bacteria
   c. both a & b
5. The image of rotaxane is shaped like a:
   a. buckyball
   b. dumbbell
   c. cube

Step 3 Solutions
1. Nanotechnology tries to make materials or machines that are:
   a. one million nanometers or larger
   b. 0.000,000,001 meter or smaller
   c. 100 nanometres or smaller
2. Most current nanotechnology work is focused on:
   a. nanoparticles with special properties
   b. surface tension
   c. DNA
3. When used as catalysts, nanoparticles and materials:
   a. produce better yields
   b. increase reaction rates
   c. both a and b
4. With nanoparticles, it is possible for:
   a. matter to disappear
   b. copper to become transparent
   c. gold to liquefy at temps below freezing
5. According to the article, one of the most interesting things about nanotechnology is:
   a. how small nanoparticles are
   b. the buckyball shape of fullerenes
   c. special properties we only see at nano scale

**Mission 7: Urban Legends**

Dear guardian friends,

If you got the message about baby spiders coming out of a girl's face, you can relax. Spiders don't lay eggs inside our bodies, and they can't live inside us. I (Ellen) am so relieved!

We are writing to ask your help in stopping the spread of urban legends like these. The stories sound like they could be true but aren't.

Complete this mission and you will be less likely to panic the next time you read an alarming message, email, or story.

Sincerely,

*Kirk, Luke, and Ellen English*
Guardians of Grammar Galaxy

## ⭐ Step 1: On Guard & Identify Urban Legends
**On Guard.** *Highlight TRUE or FALSE for each statement.*

1. Thinking about how an article applies to your life can improve you reading comprehension.  TRUE  FALSE

2. The <u>first</u> step in reading rhyming poetry is to clap as you read.  TRUE  FALSE

3. Allusions are figures of speech that aren't literal.  TRUE  FALSE

4. There are no firm guidelines for length of short stories.  TRUE  FALSE

5. Tone is the reader's attitude toward characters and events.  TRUE  FALSE

**Say each of these words in a sentence.** *Examples are given.*

| | |
|---|---|
| **convenient** – helpful | My mom says that having groceries delivered is very **convenient**. |
| **exuberant** – enthusiastic | We were **exuberant** when Dad asked if wanted to go out for ice cream. |
| **plausible** – believable | His excuse for not getting his work done seemed **plausible**. |

Mission 7: Urban Legends

**Identify urban legends.** Fact check each of the stories below using the links at GrammarGalaxyBooks.com/BlueStar. Then highlight whether each is truth or an urban legend. **Note:** Don't guess! Get the facts.

1. My friend who lives in the country enjoys cow tipping with her friends. They sneak up on sleeping cows and knock them over for fun.

    truth                  urban legend

2. If you fold a piece of paper in half 42 times, it could reach the moon.

    truth                  urban legend

3. A dwarf was bouncing on a trampoline in a circus act. He jumped sideways off the trampoline just as a hippopotamus was yawning. The dwarf was swallowed alive, and it took the audience time to realize this was wasn't part of the act.

    truth                  urban legend

4. Killswitch is a video game that can only be played once. If your character dies or you win, the game deletes itself.

    truth                  urban legend

5. Years ago, people could buy baby alligators as souvenirs in Florida. Residents of New York brought them home. When the alligators grew bigger, they flushed them down the toilet. The gators grew by feasting on rats and garbage in the sewer. They are a problem for sewer workers in New York.

    truth                  urban legend

6. It rains diamonds on Jupiter and Saturn.

    truth                  urban legend

7. The pagoda flower blooms just once every 400 years in the Himalayas.

    truth                  urban legend

8. Juliane Koepcke was the lone survivor of a Christmas Eve plane crash caused by a lightning strike. She landed, still strapped in her seat, in the Amazon rainforest after a two-mile fall from the sky.

    truth                  urban legend

⭐ Step 2: Research an Urban Legend

**Read *the urban legend about earwigs.*** *Then research so you can answer the questions that follow. Find links at GrammarGalaxyBooks.com/BlueStar.*

> My mother's friend's friend woke up one morning with a terrible headache. She went to urgent care, where they did an x-ray of her brain. The doctor determined that she had an earwig. The bug had crawled into her ear while she slept and was burrowing through her brain tissue. The doctor reassured her that it would eventually come out of her ear and the headache would go away. Until then, she was told to take over-the-counter painkillers.
>
> The bug did come out of her ear and the headache was gone. She was relieved. A week later, though, the friend's headache was back and worse than ever. She returned to urgent care and saw the same doctor. He did another x-ray of her brain and discovered that the earwig in her head had been a pregnant female. It had laid eggs in her brain and now a dozen earwigs would be working their way through her brain tissue.

1. How long has the earwig urban legend been around?

2. When are earwigs active?

3. What environment do earwigs prefer?

4. What do earwigs eat?

5. What do earwigs use their cerci for?

6. What are earwigs most attracted to inside houses?

7. How many species of earwigs are there?

8. How many eggs do females lay?


**Activity.** *Tell a family member about the spider or earwig urban legend. Then tell them the truth about the legend to reassure them. What will you say to get them to believe you?*

Mission 7: Urban Legends

☆ Step 3: Explain an Urban Legend's Appeal

**Why has the story that aliens were hidden in Area 51 in Nevada had many believers for more than 30 years?** Research Area 51 (See GrammarGalaxyBooks.com/BlueStar for links) and answer the questions below.

1. Urban legends often arise out of fear. What fears do people have about aliens and the government that keep the Area 51 legend alive?

2. Urban legends also arise from lack of information. How did lack of information help create the Area 51 legend?

3. What evidence has been given for the presence of aliens in Area 51?

4. What is the best evidence you found that there were no aliens in Area 51?

5. Do you think people will continue to believe the Area 51 legend? Why or why not?

**Vocabulary Victory!** Do you remember what these words mean? *Check Step 1 if you need a reminder.*

| convenient | It's a beautiful RV with every **convenient** feature. |
| exuberant | The children were **exuberant** as they headed to the campground in the RV. |
| plausible | Urban legends may be based on actual events or are at least **plausible**. |

Mission 7: Urban Legends

☆ Advanced Guardians Only
**Write or type your own urban legend.** *Your subject should be one that creates fear and has little information about it. Write that it happened to a friend (or friend of a friend) and include local details such as places your friends would know. You can share your legend with us, but you should only share it with others if you make it clear that you made it up!*

# OFFICIAL GUARDIAN MAIL

**Mission 7: Update**

Dear guardian friends,

Thank you for helping us get the word out about the spider story. We are hopeful that with your help, we can stop the spread of these scary stories.

However, we do want to say that the urban legends you wrote are scary, too! Make sure you don't share those, or everyone will be afraid.

Keep reassuring people with the truth. We are including the solutions to your mission.

Sincerely,

*Kirk, Luke, and Ellen English*
Guardians of Grammar Galaxy

Mission 7: Urban Legends

Step 1 Solutions

**On Guard.**

1. Thinking about how an article applies to your life can improve you reading comprehension. — TRUE FALSE
2. The first step in reading rhyming poetry is to clap as you read. — TRUE FALSE
**Instead, identify rhyming words at the ends of lines.**
3. Allusions are figures of speech that aren't literal. — TRUE FALSE
4. There are no firm guidelines for length of short stories. — TRUE FALSE
5. Tone is the reader's attitude toward characters and events. — TRUE FALSE
**Tone is the author's attitude.**

**Identify urban legends.**

1. My friend who lives in the country enjoys cow tipping with her friends. They sneak up on sleeping cows and knock them over for fun.
   truth — urban legend
2. If you fold a piece of paper in half 42 times, it could reach the moon.
   truth — urban legend
**but it would be impractical to fold a paper in half that many times**
3. A dwarf was bouncing on a trampoline in a circus act. He jumped sideways off the trampoline just as a hippopotamus was yawning. The dwarf was swallowed alive, and it took the audience time to realize this was wasn't part of the act.
   truth — urban legend
4. Killswitch is a video game that can only be played once. If your character dies or you win, the game deletes itself.
   truth — urban legend
5. Years ago, people could buy baby alligators as souvenirs in Florida. Residents of New York brought them home. When the alligators grew bigger, they flushed them down the toilet. The gators grew by feasting on rats and garbage in the sewer. They are a problem for sewer workers in New York.
   truth — urban legend
6. It rains diamonds on Jupiter and Saturn.
   truth — urban legend
7. The pagoda flower blooms just once every 400 years in the Himalayas.
   truth — urban legend
8. Juliane Koepcke was the lone survivor of a Christmas Eve plane crash caused by a lightning strike. She landed, still strapped in her seat, in the Amazon rainforest after a two-mile fall from the sky.
   truth — urban legend

Step 2 Solutions

1. How long has the earwig urban legend been around?
**Since the Middle Ages.**
2. When are earwigs active?
**At night**
3. What environment do earwigs prefer?
**Dark, moist places under things or near lights at night**
4. What do earwigs eat?
**Plants or small insects**
5. What do earwigs use their cerci for?
**Fold wings, capture prey, defend against predators**
6. What are earwigs most attracted to inside houses?
**Houseplants**
7. How many species of earwigs are there?
**2,000**
8. How many eggs do females lay?
**50-80**

Step 3 Solutions – answers will vary

1. Urban legends often arise out of fear. What fears do people have about aliens and the government that keep the Area 51 legend alive?
**Fears of alien invasion and government dishonesty**
2. Urban legends also arise from lack of information. How did lack of information help create the Area 51 legend?
**The government kept many of its activities there secret**
3. What evidence has been given for the presence of aliens in Area 51?
**UFO sightings, the book *The Roswell Incident*, and claims by Bob Lazar that he saw an alien craft and government documents about aliens**
4. What is the best evidence you found that there were no aliens in Area 51?
**Area 51 is a top-secret aircraft and counter-intelligence facility next to a nuclear testing site, providing plenty of "suspicious" activity that explains UFO sightings. There would also be more eyewitnesses to alien evidence than Bob Lazer.**

**Mission 8: Shakespeare**

Dear guardians,

    Our father is declaring this month to be Shakespeare Month. But don't worry! In this mission, you will learn how to read and enjoy Shakespearean plays.

Sincerely,
*Kirk, Luke, and Ellen English*
Guardians of Grammar Galaxy

Mission 8: Shakespeare

## ☆ Step 1: On Guard & Read Plot Synopses
**On Guard.** *Highlight TRUE or FALSE for each statement.*

1. "My friend's friend had pop rocks and soda and his stomach exploded" is probably an urban legend.   TRUE   FALSE

2. Looking at pictures and graphs can improve nonfiction reading comprehension.   TRUE   FALSE

3. You should identify emphasized syllables before reading a narrative poem aloud.   TRUE   FALSE

4. Calling a grammar mistake a Gremlin is an allusion.   TRUE   FALSE

5. More time is spent developing the plot in a short story.   TRUE   FALSE


**Say each of these words in a sentence.** *Examples are given.*

| | |
|---|---|
| **prodded** – urged | My coach **prodded** me to demonstrate the new skill for the team. |
| **notion** – idea | My cousin had the **notion** to set up an obstacle course. |
| **merely** – only | Grandma **merely** winked when I asked for a cookie. |

**Read plot synopses.** *Read the short plot summaries below. Decide which play you'd like to read. Then read a more detailed plot summary of your chosen play. Find them at GrammarGalaxyBooks.com/BlueStar.*

### A Midsummer Night's Dream

A king is preparing for his wedding when one of his noblemen asks that his daughter face potential punishment for refusing to marry the man he has chosen for her. The king gives the daughter until the time of his own wedding to agree. Meanwhile, she and the man she loves plan to run away and wed secretly. Before she does, she tells her plan to her friend. Her friend is in love with the man her father has chosen. The friend and this man follow the daughter and her intended husband into the woods to stop them.

A fairy king, who is angry with his wife, lives in the woods. He orders his servant to get the juice of a magical flower. This juice, when spread on the eyelids, causes the recipient to fall in love with the first person he sees. The servant uses the juice on the wrong people in the wrong situations, causing lots of humor and conflict.

Eventually, the daughter ends up with the man she loves and so does her friend. A group wedding is held, a funny play is enacted for entertainment, and the audience is invited to consider the whole thing a dream.

### Twelfth Night

A nobleman is in love with Lady Olivia, who refuses him because she is in mourning over her brother. Meanwhile, another young woman, Viola, survives a shipwreck, assuming her twin brother has died in it. She disguises herself as a man to get work in the nobleman's home. She falls in love with him. But Olivia falls in love with Viola, believing she is a man.

In the midst of this, Olivia's staff trick the steward into believing Olivia would be interested in him if he would act and dress in a strange fashion. This behavior gets him locked up for being insane.

Soon thereafter, Viola's twin brother arrives, alive after all. He and his sister look alike, so Olivia proposes marriage to him. He accepts. Eventually, the truth is revealed, and the nobleman realizes he loves Viola. He proposes to her. The steward is released and he leaves in a huff.

**As You Like It**

Orlando beats the court wrestler in a match. The duke's niece, Rosalind, falls in love with Orlando. But Orlando flees to the forest when he learns his older brother is trying to kill him. At the same time, the duke banishes Rosalind from his court. She also leaves for the forest with her good friend, the duke's daughter. However, Rosalind is dressed as a young man.

The duke orders Orlando's brother to find him. The duke also decides that it isn't enough that he has dethroned his own brother, Rosalind's father. He forms an army to find his brother in the forest and destroy him.

Orlando meets the duke's brother, who takes him in because his father was a friend. Orlando also finds Rosalind but assumes she's a man. The disguised Rosalind promises she can cure his lovesickness if he visits her each day. He does for some time but then stops visiting.

Orlando's brother, who was intent on killing him, arrives and explains that Orlando saved his life from a lion. Orlando's brother falls in love with Rosalind's friend, the duke's daughter. Rosalind arranges a group wedding in which she reveals her and her friend's true identities. The duke decides to return the throne to his brother after meeting a holy man. The group celebrates.

Mission 8: Shakespeare

## ⭐ Step 2: Choose the Correct Shakespearean Pronoun

**Read the sentence.** *Highlight the pronoun that belongs in the blank, ignoring capitalization.* **Hint:** <u>Thou is the subject of the sentence; thee is the object</u>.

1. _____ canst not then be false to any man.
      thou            thee

2. My love as deep; the more I give to _____.
      thou            thee

3. And for that name which is no part of _____, take all thyself.
      thou            thee

4. Shall I compare _____ to a summer's day?
      thou            thee

5. _____ art more lovely and more temperate.
      thou            thee

6. For which of my bad parts didst _____ first fall in love with me?
      thou            thee

7. If _____ sorrow, he will weep.
      thou            thee

8. He with _____ doth bear a part.
      thou            thee

**Activity.** *Watch the play or film version of the Shakespearean play you chose in Step 1.*

⭐ **Step 3: Read an Adapted/Annotated Version of a Shakespearean Play**
**See GrammarGalaxyBooks.com/BlueStar for adaptations of the play you chose in Step 1.** *Read the play. Make notes of who the characters are in the chart below. An example is given. You may continue to Chapter 9 before you finish the play.*

| Character Name | Role/Actions | Relationships |
|---|---|---|
| Duke Theseus | Preparing for marriage. Tells Hermia she must obey her father, Egeus | Marrying Hippolyta. Egeus is his cortier |
| | | |
| | | |
| | | |
| | | |
| | | |
| | | |
| | | |
| | | |

**Vocabulary Victory!** Do you remember what these words mean? *Check Step 1 if you need a reminder.*

| prodded | "Luke, what about you?" the king **prodded**. |
|---|---|
| notion | Then I have a **notion** that can change that. |
| merely | She **merely** shrugged and led the way to Luke's bedchamber. |

☆ <u>Advanced Guardians Only</u>
**Dramatize the Shakespearean play you chose with one of the options below:**
- telling the story
- acting it out with friends/family/puppets
- creating a cartoon/graphic version

Mission 8: Shakespeare

**Mission 8: Update**

Dear guardian friends,

Shakespeare Month was a hit because of you! So many of you were reading and watching Shakespearean plays. And your dramatizations even have adults checking out the books and movies from the library.

Father says he is thinking of having Shakespeare Month every year because of thee. Did you catch that Shakespearean pronoun? If you need more time to finish the play you chose, don't worry. Keep reading but begin Chapter 9 in your text. We are including the solutions to your mission.

Be not afraid of greatness,

*Kirk, Luke, and Ellen English*
Guardians of Grammar Galaxy

Mission 8: Shakespeare

Step 1 Solutions
**On Guard.**
1. "My friend's friend had pop rocks and soda and his stomach exploded" is probably an urban legend. — **TRUE** FALSE
2. Looking at pictures and graphs can improve nonfiction reading comprehension. — **TRUE** FALSE
3. You should identify emphasized syllables before reading a narrative poem aloud. — **TRUE** FALSE
4. Calling a grammar mistake a Gremlin is an allusion. — **TRUE** FALSE
5. More time is spent developing the plot in a short story. — TRUE **FALSE**

Step 2 Solutions

1. _____ canst not then be false to any man.
   **thou** / thee
2. My love as deep; the more I give to _____.
   thou / **thee**
3. And for that name which is no part of _____, take all thyself.
   thou / **thee**
4. Shall I compare _____ to a summer's day?
   thou / **thee**
5. _____ art more lovely and more temperate.
   **thou** / thee
6. For which of my bad parts didst _____ first fall in love with me?
   **thou** / thee
7. If _____ sorrow, he will weep.
   **thou** / thee
8. He with _____ doth bear a part.
   thou / **thee**

**Mission 9: Satire**

Dear guardians,

You might have read an article about our father that has you upset. It was published on a site that says it's about news. But it turns out that the article was satire. That means it's not factual, and it was intended to be funny.

We want you to be able to recognize satire when you read it, so we are sending you this mission to complete. And don't worry! We don't have a camera in your house, watching to make sure you complete it. Promise!

Sincerely,

*Kirk, Luke, and Ellen English*
Guardians of Grammar Galaxy

## ⭐ Step 1: On Guard & Identify the Type of Satire

**On Guard.** *Highlight the correct answer for each statement or blank.*

1. A good way to understand Shakespeare is to watch the play:
   while sleeping     before reading     after reading

2. Urban legends often arise from lack of information and:
   fear               boredom            humor

3. Looking at nonfiction subtitles _____ your mind.
   frees              confuses           primes

4. "Casey at the Bat" is a _____ poem.
   nonfiction         narrative          allusion

5. An allusion is a figure of _____.
   speech             words              math


**Say each of these words in a sentence.** *Examples are given.*

| **binges** – sprees | Grandpa enjoys movie **binges** on a rainy day. |
|---|---|
| **flabbergasted** – stunned | We were **flabbergasted** that we won the prize drawing. |
| **verify** – confirm | My mom likes to **verify** that I've done my work. |

**Identify the type of satire.** *For each cartoon, highlight whether it is a parody, diminution, inflation, or juxtaposition.*

"Juice box?"

1. parody     diminution     inflation     juxtaposition

"What have you two been doing all day?"

2. parody     diminution     inflation     juxtaposition

"Dr. Pat, can I buy a vowel?"

3. parody     diminution     inflation     juxtaposition

Mission 9: Satire

⭐ Step 2: Identify Article Titles That are Most Likely Satire
**Read the article title.** *If it is most likely an article poking fun, highlight satire. Otherwise, highlight "not satire."*

1. "The President: 'Our Long National Nightmare of Peace and Prosperity is Over'"
   satire          not satire

2. "Lots of Frogs and Salamanders Have a Secret Glow"
   satire          not satire

3. "Legos Could Last a Disturbingly Long Time in the Ocean"
   satire          not satire

4. "Scientists Continue Developing Alternative Energy Sources for People to Waste"

   satire          not satire

5. "'I Am Under 18' Button Clicked for First Time in History of Internet"
   satire          not satire

6. "A Seventh Grader Named NASA's Newest Mars Rover"
   satire          not satire

7. "World Death Rate Holding Steady at 100 Percent"
   satire          not satire

8. "Friends of Band Regret Going to Show"
   satire          not satire

**Activity.** Read a satirical children's book. See GrammarGalaxyBooks.com/BlueStar for recommended titles.

Mission 9: Satire

## ⭐ Step 3: Identify the Meaning in Satirical Quotes

For each satirical *Calvin & Hobbes* quote below, write what you think author Bill Watterson is trying to communicate.

1. "Becoming an adult is probably the dumbest thing you could ever do!"

_____

2. "No, I'm going to whine until I get the special treatment I like."

_____

3. "You know, it's amazing how many things you can take apart with just one ordinary screwdriver."

_____

4. "In my book, food should be nutrition **and** entertainment."

_____

5. "The problem with tigers is they have no setting between 'off' and 'high.'"

_____

6. "Oh, here it is! Who put it in the stupid closet?!?"

_____

7. "Given that, sooner or later, we're all just going to die, what's the point of learning about integers?"

_____

8. "You know you'll hate something when they won't tell you what it is."

_____

**Vocabulary Victory!** Do you remember what these words mean? *Check Step 1 if you need a reminder.*

| binges | Is Mother on one of her cleaning **binges**? |
| flabbergasted | Luke read slowly and seemed **flabbergasted**. |
| verify | They have to **verify** their facts. |

Mission 9: Satire

⭐ <u>Advanced Guardians Only</u>

**Weird Al Yankovic is famous for writing song parodies, like "Eat It" for Michael Jackson's "Beat It."** *Choose one of the children's songs below, highlight it, and write a new, humorous version of it. Go to GrammarGalaxyBooks.com/ BlueStar if you need the original lyrics.*

- "The Wheels on the Bus"
- "If You're Happy and You Know It"
- "Old MacDonald Had a Farm"

New Song Title _____

# OFFICIAL GUARDIAN MAIL

**Mission 9: Update**

Dear guardians,

    We hope that completing this mission has helped you tell the difference between satire and factual reporting. The article about our father was exaggerated and funny, once we realized it wasn't true!

    We sure enjoyed the parody songs you wrote. We've been singing some of them!

    We are including the solutions to this mission and a Literature Challenge for you to complete. We know you will do well on it! See you in Unit II.

Sincerely,

*Kirk, Luke, and Ellen English*
Guardians of Grammar Galaxy

Step 1 Solutions
**On Guard.**
1. A good way to understand Shakespeare is to watch the play:
while sleeping    before reading    after reading
2. Urban legends often arise from lack of information and:
fear    boredom    humor
3. Looking at nonfiction subtitles _____ your mind.
frees    confuses    primes
4. "Casey at the Bat" is a _____ poem.
nonfiction    narrative    allusion
5. An allusion is a figure of _____.
speech    words    math

**Identify the type of satire.**
1. diminution – the boxer is being treated like a child
2. inflation – the snowman is huge
3. parody – poking fun at *Wheel of Fortune* (which is also an allusion)

Step 2 Solutions
1. "The President: 'Our Long National Nightmare of Peace and Prosperity is Over'"
    satire    not satire
2. "Lots of Frogs and Salamanders Have a Secret Glow"
    satire    not satire
3. "Legos Could Last a Disturbingly Long Time in the Ocean"
    satire    not satire
4. "Scientists Continue Developing Alternative Energy Sources for People to Waste"
    satire    not satire
5. "'I Am Under 18' Button Clicked for First Time in History of Internet"
    satire    not satire
6. "A Seventh Grader Named NASA's Newest Mars Rover"
    satire    not satire
7. "World Death Rate Holding Steady at 100 Percent"
    satire    not satire
8. "Friends of Band Regret Going to Show"
    satire    not satire

Step 3 Solutions – answers will vary
1. "Becoming an adult is probably the dumbest thing you could ever do!"
**Childhood is fun and carefree, while adulthood can be challenging.**
2. "No, I'm going to whine until I get the special treatment I like."
**Kids are rewarded for whining and thus don't stop.**
3. "You know, it's amazing how many things you can take apart with just one ordinary screwdriver."
**Kids can take apart and ruin things unintentionally.**
4. "In my book, food should be nutrition **and** entertainment."
**Kids don't like healthy food that doesn't taste good.**
5. "The problem with tigers is they have no setting between 'off' and 'high.'"
**Tigers, like kids, are either resting or playing hard.**
6. "Oh, here it is! Who put it in the stupid closet?!?"
**We blame people for "losing" our things, even when they are properly put away.**
7. "Given that, sooner or later, we're all just going to die, what's the point of learning about integers?"
**Kids often believe that advanced math doesn't help us in life.**
8. "You know you'll hate something when they won't tell you what it is."
**When adults keep secrets, it may be because kids won't be happy about it.**

# Literature Challenge I

*Carefully read all the possible answers* and then highlight the letter for the **one** best answer.

1. **A subject typically included in a literature unit study is:**
   a. math
   b. art
   c. neither a nor b

2. **Tone is the author's attitude toward:**
   a. the characters
   b. events
   c. both a and b

3. **A short story is usually no more than:**
   a. 4,000 words
   b. 1,000 words
   c. 40,000 words

4. **An allusion is:**
   a. direct
   b. indirect
   c. always nonfiction

5. **Narrative poems:**
   a. are always long
   b. are always set to music
   c. tell stories

6. **Before reading nonfiction, you should:**
   a. read subtitles
   b. take a nap
   c. make a personal connection with the text

7. **Urban legends arise from:**
   a. fear
   b. lack of information
   c. both a and b

8. **Shakespeare used _____ as a subject pronoun.**
   a. thee
   b. thou
   c. both a and b

9. **The book *Goodnight iPad* is an example of:**
   a. parody
   b. inflation
   c. juxtaposition

10. **Mood is created in:**
    a. setting
    b. illustrations
    c. both a and b

Number Correct:_____/10

Literature Challenge

## ⭐ *Advanced Guardian Vocabulary Challenge*
For an extra challenge, highlight the word that best fits each blank.

1. **My friend _____ declared that she'd gotten a perfect score.**
   merely          sanctimoniously          absent-mindedly

2. **The punishment for a low score is too harsh for such a small _____.**
   narcissist          notion          infraction

3. **My mother said I needed to stop _____ about the test.**
   ruminating          gratifying          indifference

4. **She said I scored poorly because I was _____ about studying.**
   exuberant          engaged          halfhearted

5. **I think my chances of getting a good score are _____.**
   convenient          dismal          cultural

6. **My friends' reports of getting perfect scores do not seem _____.**
   verify          prodded          plausible

7. **My mother explained that study _____ do not work.**
   binges          sanctions          pall

8. **"There are more important matters in life than test scores," she said _____.**
   exuberant          jauntily          flabberghasted

Number Correct: _____/8

Literature Challenge

★ Advanced Guardian Vocabulary Challenge
For an extra challenge, highlight the word that best fits each blank.

1. My friend _____ declared that she'd gotten a perfect score.
   merrily          sanctimoniously          absent-mindedly

2. The punishment for a low score is too harsh for such a small _____.
   bourgeois          notion          infraction

3. My mother said I needed to stop _____ about the test.
   lamenting          gratifying          the fleece

4. She said I scored poorly because I was _____ about studying.
   adamant          engaged          nonchalant

5. I think my chances of getting a good score are _____.
   convenient          dismal          illusory

6. My friend's report of getting perfect scores does not seem _____.
   verily          engaged          plausible

7. My mother explained that study _____ do not work.
   binges          tantrums          polls

8. "There are more important matters in life than test scores," she said.
   vex herant          disputify          flabbergasted

   Numbered _____ 18

Literature Challenge 1 Answers
1.b; 2.c; 3.a; 4.b; 5.c; 6.a; 7.c; 8.b; 9.a; 10.c

**If you got 9 or more correct, congratulations!** You've earned your Literature star. You may add it to your Grammar Guardian bookmark. You can print a bookmark on cardstock with your teacher's help on cardstock from GrammarGalaxyBooks.com/BlueStar. You are ready for an adventure in spelling and vocabulary.

**If you did not get 9 or more correct, don't worry.** You have another chance. You may want to review the information in the guidebook for each story you've read so far. Then take the Literature Challenge 2. Remember to **choose the one best answer**.

Advanced Guardian Vocabulary Challenge Answers
1. sanctimoniously
2. infraction
3. ruminating
4. halfhearted
5. dismal
6. plausible
7. binges
8. jauntily

Literature Challenge

# Literature Challenge 2

*Carefully read all the possible answers* and then highlight the letter for the **one** best answer.

1. **Studying multiple subjects related to the book *Island of the Blue Dolphins* is called a:**
   a. literature unit study
   b. novel study
   c. either a or b

2. **"Gloomy cliffs, so worn and wasted with the washing of the waves" has a mood of:**
   a. dark, depressing
   b. mocking, teasing
   c. cheery, bright

3. **In short stories, <u>less</u> time is spent developing the:**
   a. plot
   b. mood
   c. illustrations

4. **A father who says, "One small step for man, one giant leap for our family" is using an:**
   a. illusion
   b. allusion
   c. reference

5. **The poem "April Showers" from the story is best described as:**
   a. an epic
   b. satire
   c. a ballad

6. **Recalling a documentary on the moon landing while reading an article on the preservation of moon rocks will improve:**
   a. your typing speed
   b. your fiction reading comprehension
   c. your nonfiction reading comprehension

7. **The story of baby spiders hatching from a friend's cheek is:**
   a. satire
   b. an urban legend
   c. a Shakespeare plot

8. **One way to understand and enjoy Shakespeare is:**
   a. see a play before reading it
   b. read an annotated version of the play
   c. either a or b

9. **A cartoon of a politician with an enormous nose is an example of:**
   a. inflation
   b. parody
   c. juxtaposition

10. **An email about Bigfoot is most likely:**
    a. satire
    b. a short story
    c. an urban legend

Number Correct:_____/10

Literature Challenge

Literature Challenge 2 Answers
1.c; 2.a; 3.a; 4.b; 5.c; 6.c; 7.b; 8.c; 9.a; 10.c

**If you got 9 or more correct, congratulations!** You've earned your Literature star. You may add a star to your bookmark. You can print a bookmark on cardstock with your teacher's help from GrammarGalaxyBooks.com/BlueStar.

**If you did not get 9 or more correct, don't worry.** Review the questions you missed with your teacher. You may want to get more practice using the resources at GrammarGalaxyBooks.com/BlueStar. Your teacher can ask you other questions like the ones you missed and if you get them correct, you'll have earned your Literature star and can move on to an adventure in spelling and vocabulary.

# Unit II: Adventures in Spelling & Vocabulary

# OFFICIAL GUARDIAN MAIL

**Mission 10: Science Vocabulary**

Dear astronomical guardians,

Some time ago, we learned that *astr* means star. You're certainly stars in this galaxy!

Are you planning on participating in the science fair? If so, learning science vocabulary can make doing your project and your other science studies much easier. That's why we are sending you this mission. We hope you think it's a dynamite one—in other words, a powerful mission.

You will need the Word Root list we are including.

Sincerely,

*Kirk, Luke, and Ellen English*
Guardians of Grammar Galaxy

## Common Greek & Latin Science Word Roots

| Root | Meaning | Root | Meaning |
|---|---|---|---|
| spect | see, observe | vac | empty |
| hydr | water | chron | time |
| therm | heat | bene | good |
| aqu | water | dyna | power |
| kinesis | movement | syn | with, together |
| ab | move away | circ | round |
| duc | lead, make | gen | to birth |
| lev | to lift | luc, lum | light |
| omni | all | bio | life |

Mission 10: Science Vocabulary

⭐ Step 1: On Guard & Match the Word to Its Meaning

**On Guard.** *Answer the questions or answer them verbally for your teacher.*

1. What is satire?

2. Who was Shakespeare?

3. What is an urban legend?

4. What is one way to better understand a nonfiction article?

5. What is a narrative poem?

**Say each of these words in a sentence.** *Examples are given.*

| longingly – desirously | My dog was looking **longingly** at my eggs. |
|---|---|
| sputtering – stammering | My dad was so surprised that he was **sputtering** his thank you. |
| suppressed – repressed | We **suppressed** our excitement about the win until the other team left. |

**Match the word to its meaning.** *Draw a line from the science vocabulary word to its likely meaning.* **Hint:** <u>Use the root word list we sent you before looking words up in the dictionary.</u>

| | |
|---|---|
| hydrothermal | timepiece |
| omnivore | putting together |
| abduction | eats all food |
| vacuole | takes water away |
| chronometer | go around |
| synthesis | taking away |
| circumvent | heated water |
| translucent | force |
| leverage | space inside a cell |
| aqueduct | light shows through |

Mission 10: Science Vocabulary

⭐ Step 2: Choose the Correct Vocabulary Word

**Read each sentence.** *Then highlight the science vocabulary word that belongs in the blank.* **Hint:** *Review the root word meanings to determine if each word makes sense.*

1. To make sure we arrived together, we _____ our watches.
   microphoned          synchronized          photosynthesized

2. Because Luke hates to sit still, Mother says he is a _____ learner.
   aquatic              astrologic            kinesthetic

3. The queen doesn't like dark rooms and is always seeking to _____ them.
   illuminate           levitate              omniscient

4. At chore time, the queen insists we _____ our beds immediately.
   deduce               levitate              vacate

5. The king enjoys having the windows open so the air can _____.
   circulate            generate              abstain

6. The king wants to be known as a ruler and a _____.
   omnivore             generator             benefactor

7. Because the queen didn't agree with the king, she chose to _____ from sharing her opinion.
   deduce               abstain               spectate

8. The queen told Luke he didn't need his _____ underwear for their beach trip.
   thermal              dynamic               kinetic


**Activity.** *Do an Archimedes science experiment to learn about buoyancy. See GrammarGalaxyBooks.com/BlueStar for instructions.*

## ⭐ Step 3: Do Some Science Reading and Record New Vocabulary Words

**Read a science book or article.** *When you come to a new vocabulary word, record it in your word book. Make copies of the following pages or download them at GrammarGalaxyBooks.com/BlueStar.*

**Vocabulary Victory!** Do you remember what these words mean? *Check Step 1 if you need a reminder.*

| longingly | "I don't think it's a big deal," the king said, looking **longingly** at his newspaper. |
|---|---|
| sputtering | The queen turned and left, leaving the king **sputtering**. |
| suppressed | She buried her head in her pillow and the king **suppressed** a laugh. |

# Words Learned Since _____

New Word  _____

    Synonym:

    Definition:


New Word  _____

    Synonym:

    Definition:


New Word  _____

    Synonym:

    Definition:


New Word  _____

    Synonym:

    Definition:

Mission 10: Science Vocabulary

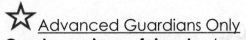 Advanced Guardians Only

**Create a science fair entry.** *Learn about an area of science you're interested in. Create a display or demonstration. Be sure to display the new words you've learned as part of your research.*

# OFFICIAL GUARDIAN MAIL

**Mission 10: Update**

Dear thermoriffic guardians,

That's our way of saying you're on fire! We loved seeing the new science words you're learning. And your science fair entries were fascinating, too. Did you get wet doing the buoyancy experiment like we did?

We are including the solutions to this mission. We hope you keep adding new vocabulary words to your Word Book.

Sincerely,

*Kirk, Luke, and Ellen English*
Guardians of Grammar Galaxy

Mission 10: Science Vocabulary

Step 1 Solutions

**On Guard**. – *answers do not have to be exact*

1. What is satire?
Satire is the use of humor, irony, or exaggeration to poke fun in a good-natured way.
2. Who was Shakespeare?
William Shakespeare is often called the greatest English writer of all time. He lived in England from the late 1500s to the early 1600s. He wrote 39 plays and many poems. He was also an actor with the nickname of "the Bard."
3. What is an urban legend?
Urban legends are scary or funny fictional stories presented as true tales.
4. What is one way to better understand a nonfiction article?
Skimming the title and a short section of text; glancing at subtitles and any images or graphs. Asking yourself what the article or chapter is about. Asking yourself what you already know about the subject. Considering the importance of the information for your life or the world.
5. What is a narrative poem?
Poems that tell stories in verses and often use rhythm and rhyme.

**Match the word to its meaning.**

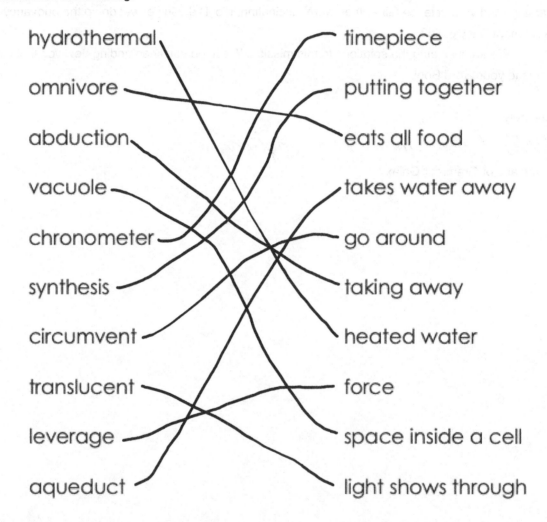

Step 2 Solutions

1. To make sure we arrived together, we _____ our watches.
   microphoned    synchronized    photosynthesized
2. Because Luke hates to sit still, Mother says he is a _____ learner.
   aquatic    astrologic    kinesthetic
3. The queen doesn't like dark rooms and is always seeking to _____ them.
   illuminate    levitate    omniscient

Mission 10: Science Vocabulary

4. At chore time, the queen insists we _____ our beds immediately.
   deduce          levitate          vacate
5. The king enjoys having the windows open so the air can _____.
   circulate       generate          abstain
6. The king wants to be known as a ruler and a _____.
   omnivore        generator         benefactor
7. Because the queen didn't agree with the king, she chose to _____ from sharing her opinion.
   deduce          abstain           spectate
8. The queen told Luke he didn't need his _____ underwear for their beach trip.
   **thermal**         dynamic           kinetic

Mission 10: Science Vocabulary

# OFFICIAL GUARDIAN MAIL

**Mission 11: Oxymorons**

Dear guardian friends,

It's an open secret that parents love the new comedian Oxymoron. His popularity has resulted in the overuse of oxymorons, which are contradictory figures of speech. Our only choice is to get you guardians using them a lot. As a result, we expect Oxymoron will bring in small crowds of people who offer him deafening silence. With your help completing this mission, we hope to give him a farewell reception.

Sincerely,

*Kirk, Luke, and Ellen English*
Guardians of Grammar Galaxy

## ⭐ Step 1: On Guard & Identify Oxymorons

**On Guard.** *Highlight the correct answer.*

1. A science word meaning 'movement of heat through an object' is:
   aqueous          conduction          luminous

2. A political cartoon of a leader drawn small is an example of:
   inflation          juxtaposition          diminution

3. The first step in understanding Shakespeare is to read:
   a plot summary          an annotated play          the original play

4. Which of these is an urban legend?
   killer bees          ticks carrying disease          gators in sewers

5. To better understand *Grammar Galaxy*, first look at:
   vocabulary words          your watch          the number of pages

**Say each of these words in a sentence.** *Examples are given.*

| **charmed** – pleased | The author said she was **charmed** to meet my mother. |
|---|---|
| **incongruity** – oddness | The **incongruity** of seeing my dad dressed as a cowboy made me laugh. |
| **vogue** – fashion | Mullet hairstyles are no longer in **vogue**. |

**Identify oxymorons.** There are five oxymorons in our letter to you. *Highlight them.*

## ⭐ Step 2: Identify Oxymorons in the Comedian's Set

**The comedian Oxymoron used 12 oxymorons when teasing the king and queen.** *Highlight them in the text below.*

"You obviously wanted to have a night alone together," the comedian said. "Just you and a small crowd hanging out together."

The king laughed. He wanted to say, "Exactly! Not what I had in mind for a date," but he said nothing.

"Well, we want you two to have an awful good time, right?" he asked the audience. They responded with hoots and applause.

"How long have you two been married?" he asked the king.

The king hesitated, unsettled by the attention. "Fourteen years?" he said as a question.

"That sounds like a definite maybe to me," Oxymoron teased. The king smiled ruefully.

"With him not knowing for sure how long you've been married, it's a minor miracle you're still together. Am I right?" the comedian asked the queen.

The queen nodded, laughing. The king was not happy with her response.

"But I guess if you want to be a queen, he's your only choice," he said. The queen and the rest of the audience laughed. The king reddened.

"I better be careful. This might be a working vacation for our king. I want to use terribly good grammar, or I'll suddenly be found missing." The audience laughed, but the king's mouth was set in a hard line.

"Hey, some true fiction about our king for you. I have it from a source inside the palace that the code name they use for him is Jumbo Shrimp. His super-secret code name is the Larger Half."

**Activity.** *Try to use as many oxymorons in your conversation today as possible. Does anyone notice?*

Mission 11: Oxymorons

## ⭐ Step 3: Use an Oxymoron in the Sentences
**Write an oxymoron from the box that makes sense in the sentence.** Add it to the blank.

| | | |
|---|---|---|
| bittersweet | walking dead | passive aggressive |
| random order | jumbo shrimp | act naturally |
| seriously funny | exact estimate | awfully lucky |
| unpopular celebrities | unbiased opinion | friendly fire |

1. The king tried to _____ during the comedy show.

2. The queen thought Oxymoron was _____.

3. The king hoped Oxymoron would eventually be another of those _____.

4. The king was so tired after their night out, he felt like the _____.

5. Before agreeing to see the comedian, the king wanted an _____ of the ticket prices.

6. The king thought the comedian was being _____ toward him.

7. In the king's _____, Oxymoron was not that funny.

8. Oxymoron wrote the king to say that he hoped no offense was taken and to consider his jokes _____.

**Vocabulary Victory!** Do you remember what these words mean? *Check Step 1 if you need a reminder.*

| charmed | The king was **charmed** with his wife. |
|---|---|
| incongruity | Recognition of the **incongruity** of the oxymoron may be lost. |
| vogue | Oxymoron is in **vogue**, right? |

Mission 11: Oxymorons

## ☆ Advanced Guardians Only

**Write about one of the paradoxes below.** Highlight your choice. Then explain how you've seen the truth of the paradox in your own life. Type or hand-write your response.

- If I know anything, it's that I know nothing.
- Don't go near the water 'til you have learned how to swim.
- "I can resist anything but temptation." – Oscar Wilde

Mission 11: Oxymorons

# OFFICIAL GUARDIAN MAIL

**Mission 11: Update**

Dear guardians,

You made that look like an easy challenge. Whoops! We're still using oxymorons sometimes. But our mission appears to be working. Oxymoron's shows were so crowded that no one goes to see him anymore.

We are including the solutions to your mission.

Gratefully,

*Kirk, Luke, and Ellen English*
Guardians of Grammar Galaxy

Mission 11: Oxymorons

Step 1 Solutions

**On Guard**.

1. A science word meaning 'movement of heat through an object' is:
   aqueous    **conduction**    luminous

2. A political cartoon of a leader drawn small is an example of:
   inflation    juxtaposition    **diminution**

3. The first step in understanding Shakespeare is to read:
   **a plot summary**    an annotated play    the original play

4. Which of these is an urban legend?
   killer bees    ticks carrying disease    **gators in sewers**

5. To better understand *Grammar Galaxy*, first look at:
   **vocabulary words**    your watch    the number of pages

**Identify oxymorons**.

Dear guardian friends,
   It's an *open secret* that parents love the new comedian Oxymoron. His popularity has resulted in the overuse of oxymorons, which are contradictory figures of speech. Our *only choice* is to get you guardians using them a lot. As a result, we expect Oxymoron will bring in *small crowds* of people who offer him *deafening silence*. With your help completing this mission, we hope to give him a *farewell reception*.

Step 2 Solutions

   "You obviously wanted to have a night *alone together*," the comedian said. "Just you and a *small crowd* hanging out together."
   The king laughed. He wanted to say, "Exactly! Not what I had in mind for a date," but he said nothing.
   "Well, we want you two to have an *awful good* time, right?" he asked the audience. They responded with hoots and applause.
   "How long have you two been married?" he asked the king.
   The king hesitated, unsettled by the attention. "Fourteen years?" he said as a question.
   "That sounds like a *definite maybe* to me," Oxymoron teased. The king smiled ruefully.
   "With him not knowing for sure how long you've been married, it's a *minor miracle* you're still together. Am I right?" the comedian asked the queen.
   The queen nodded, laughing. The king was not happy with her response.
   "But I guess if you want to be a queen, he's your *only choice*," he said. The queen and the rest of the audience laughed. The king reddened.
   "I better be careful. This might be a *working vacation* for our king. I want to use *terribly good* grammar, or I'll suddenly be *found missing*." The audience laughed, but the king's mouth was set in a hard line.
   "Hey, some *true fiction* about our king for you. I have it from a source inside the palace that the code name they use for him is *Jumbo Shrimp*. His super-secret code name is the *Larger Half*."

Step 3 Solutions

1. The king tried to <u>act naturally</u> during the comedy show.

2. The queen thought Oxymoron was <u>seriously funny</u>.

3. The king hoped Oxymoron would eventually be another of those <u>unpopular celebrities</u>.

4. The king was so tired after their night out, he felt like the <u>walking dead</u>.

5. Before agreeing to see the comedian, the king wanted an <u>exact estimate</u> of the ticket prices.

6. The king thought the comedian was being <u>passive aggressive</u> toward him.

7. In the king's <u>unbiased opinion</u>, Oxymoron was not that funny.

8. Oxymoron wrote the king to say that he hoped no offense was taken and to consider his jokes <u>friendly fire</u>.

# OFFICIAL GUARDIAN MAIL

**Mission 12: Onomatopoeia**

Dear guardians,

Likely you've heard about the tram accident. We are okay and the Transportation Authority is investigating the cause.

But something else was strange about the accident. We didn't hear anything! Our father determined that this is because the Onomatopoeia Union is on strike on planet Vocabulary. They believe they are unfairly doing two jobs.

We need your help to identify onomatopoeia words, so we can contact them. We will explain that they will only be asked to do one job (noun or verb) at a time. We hope that they will end their strike as a result. Complete this mission so we can hear sounds like our dog Comet's bark once again.

Sincerely,

*Kirk, Luke, and Ellen English*
Guardians of Grammar Galaxy

Mission 12: Onomatopoeia

## ⭐ Step 1: On Guard & Highlight Onomatopoeia
**On Guard.** *Highlight the correct answer.*

1. Jumbo shrimp is an:
   onomatopoeia    oxymoron    urban legend

2. The word root *omni* means:
   all    none    some

3. Weird Al Yankovic is famous for creating:
   onomatopoeia    urban legends    parodies

4. One of Shakespeare's famous plays is:
   Twelfth Night    Tenth Night    Eleventh Night

5. Before sharing a story that a friend told you:
   make it your own    check the facts    add some satire

**Say each of these words in a sentence.** *Examples are given.*

| | |
|---|---|
| **shaken** – traumatized | My mother was **shaken** by the news of her friend's illness. |
| **soothe** – calm | My father tried to **soothe** my baby sister. |
| **numbly** – dazedly | I was so tired that I **numbly** brushed my teeth. |

Mission 12: Onomatopoeia

**Highlight onomatopoeia words in the poem "The Bells" by Edgar Allen Poe.** The rhythm of this poem is itself onomatopoeia, reminding us of bell ringing. You'll even find the author's last name in the word onoma**topoe**ia! Highlight each word from the word box below where you find it in the poem.

| | | | | | |
|---|---|---|---|---|---|
| tinkle | jingling | tinkling | ring | ringing | gloats |
| gush | scream | shriek | clang | clash | roar |
| twanging | clanging | jangling | chiming | palpitating | clangor |
| groan | tolling | muffled | moaning | groaning | |

### I.

Hear the sledges with the bells—
Silver bells!
What a world of merriment their melody foretells!
How they tinkle, tinkle, tinkle,
In the icy air of night!
While the stars that oversprinkle
All the heavens, seem to twinkle
With a crystalline delight;
 Keeping time, time, time,
In a sort of Runic rhyme,
To the tintinabulation that so musically wells
From the bells, bells, bells, bells,
Bells, bells, bells—
From the jingling and the tinkling of the bells.

### II.

Hear the mellow wedding bells,
Golden bells!
What a world of happiness their harmony foretells!
Through the balmy air of night
How they ring out their delight!
From the molten-golden notes,
And all in tune,
What a liquid ditty floats
To the turtle-dove that listens, while she gloats
On the moon!
Oh, from out the sounding cells,
What a gush of euphony voluminously wells!
How it swells!
How it dwells
On the Future! how it tells
Of the rapture that impels
To the swinging and the ringing
Of the bells, bells, bells,
Of the bells, bells, bells, bells,
Bells, bells, bells—
To the rhyming and the chiming of the bells!

### III.

Hear the loud alarum bells—
Brazen bells!
What tale of terror, now, their turbulency tells!
In the startled ear of night
How they scream out their affright!
Too much horrified to speak,
They can only shriek, shriek,
Out of tune,
In a clamorous appealing to the mercy of the fire,
In a mad expostulation with the deaf and frantic fire,
Leaping higher, higher, higher,
With a desperate desire,
And a resolute endeavor
Now—now to sit or never,
By the side of the pale-faced moon.
Oh, the bells, bells, bells!
What a tale their terror tells
Of Despair!
How they clang, and clash, and roar!
What a horror they outpour
On the bosom of the palpitating air!
Yet the ear it fully knows,
By the twanging,
And the clanging,
How the danger ebbs and flows;
Yet the ear distinctly tells,
In the jangling,
And the wrangling.
How the danger sinks and swells,
By the sinking or the swelling in the anger of the bells—
Of the bells—
Of the bells, bells, bells, bells,
Bells, bells, bells—
In the clamor and the clangor of the bells!

(continue next page)

**IV.**
Hear the tolling of the bells—
Iron bells!
What a world of solemn thought their monody compels!
In the silence of the night,
How we shiver with affright
At the melancholy menace of their tone!
For every sound that floats
From the rust within their throats
Is a groan.
And the people—ah, the people—
They that dwell up in the steeple,
All alone,
And who tolling, tolling, tolling,
In that muffled monotone,
Feel a glory in so rolling
On the human heart a stone—
They are neither man nor woman—
They are neither brute nor human—
They are Ghouls:
And their king it is who tolls;
And he rolls, rolls, rolls,
Rolls
A pæan from the bells!
And his merry bosom swells
With the pæan of the bells!
And he dances, and he yells;
Keeping time, time, time,
In a sort of Runic rhyme,
To the pæan of the bells—
Of the bells:
Keeping time, time, time,
In a sort of Runic rhyme,
To the throbbing of the bells—
Of the bells, bells, bells—
To the sobbing of the bells;
Keeping time, time, time,
As he knells, knells, knells,
In a happy Runic rhyme,
To the rolling of the bells—
Of the bells, bells, bells—
To the tolling of the bells,
Of the bells, bells, bells, bells—
Bells, bells, bells—
To the moaning and the groaning of the bells.

**Note:** A pæan is a song or lyric poem of triumph or gratitude.

Mission 12: Onomatopoeia

## ⭐ Step 2: Associate Onomatopoeia Sounds
**For each item, highlight one onomatopoeia sound it is likely to make.** *Note: The word has to represent a sound.*

1. **helicopter**
   lift      whir      takeoff

2. **goose**
   honk      whisper      fly

3. **faucet**
   run      leak      drip

4. **child**
   hiccup      yell      laugh

5. **shoe**
   fit      flashy      squeak

6. **plate**
   clatter      full      stack

7. **leaves**
   change      rustle      bud

8. **bird**
   song      nest      tweet


**Activity.** *Read a poem with onomatopoeia aloud. You may read "The Bells" or one of the poems you can find linked at GrammarGalaxyBooks.com/ BlueStar.*

Mission 12: Onomatopoeia

## ⭐ Step 3: Write an Onomatopoeia Word in the Blank
**Read the sentence and write a sound word in the blank from the word box that makes sense.**

| sizzle | clink | giggle | splash | mumble |
| bawl | neigh | thump | dribble | swoosh |

1. The English children's favorite part of the water slide is the _____ at the end.

2. Luke loves the _____ of dropping coins into his piggy bank.

3. When Kirk watches basketball, he loves hearing the _____ of the basketball through the net.

4. Ellen loves a horse's _____ when she greets one.

5. The queen doesn't like it when the children _____.

6. The king loves hearing the _____ of food in a frying pan.

7. The hose was kinked so the sound of the water coming out was just a _____.

8. When the king tripped over the hose, the children couldn't help but _____.


**Vocabulary Victory!** Do you remember what these words mean? *Check Step 1 if you need a reminder.*

| shaken | I imagine you're all a little **shaken** by this experience. |
|---|---|
| soothe | Talking about it will **soothe** you. |
| numbly | The children **numbly** shook their heads. |

Mission 12: Onomatopoeia

## ☆ Advanced Guardians Only
**Write a descriptive poem or paragraph using onomatopoeia.** *First, choose a subject. Then write as many sound words as you can think of to describe it. Finally, type or write your descriptive poem or paragraph. Review the poems linked at GrammarGalaxyBooks.com/BlueStar for inspiration.*

Subject_____

Onomatopoeia words that describe it:



Poem or Paragraph

_____
_____
_____
_____
_____
_____
_____
_____
_____
_____
_____
_____
_____
_____
_____
_____
_____
_____
_____
_____
_____

Mission 12: Onomatopoeia

# OFFICIAL GUARDIAN MAIL

**Mission 12: Update**

Dear guardians,

We can hear Comet bark! Yes, with your help, we were able to convince the Onomatopoeia Union to call off the strike. Plop, plop, fizz, fizz, oh, what a relief that is! (That's from an old commercial that used onomatopoeia.)

We also have news about the tram accident. A mouse had gotten into the power grid for the tram and damaged it. Perhaps the lack of sound words (e.g., squeak) kept it from being discovered. Fortunately, the tram is being repaired and we will be able to reschedule our science center trip.

We are including the solutions to your mission for your review. Thank you so much for your help.

Sincerely,

*Kirk, Luke, and Ellen English*
Guardians of Grammar Galaxy

Mission 12: Onomatopoeia

Step 1 Solutions

**On Guard.**

1. Jumbo shrimp is an:
   onomatopoeia          **oxymoron**          urban legend
2. The word root *omni* means:
   **all**               none                  some
3. Weird Al Yankovic is famous for creating:
   onomatopoeia          urban legends         **parodies**
4. One of Shakespeare's famous plays is:
   **Twelfth Night**     Tenth Night           Eleventh Night
5. Before sharing a story that a friend told you:
   make it your own      **check the facts**   add some satire

**Highlight onomatopoeia.**

I.
Hear the sledges with the bells—
Silver bells!
What a world of merriment their melody foretells!
How they **tinkle, tinkle, tinkle**,
In the icy air of night!
While the stars that oversprinkle
All the heavens, seem to twinkle
With a crystalline delight;
Keeping time, time, time,
In a sort of Runic rhyme,
To the tintinabulation that so musically wells
From the bells, bells, bells, bells,
Bells, bells, bells—
From the **jingling** and the **tinkling** of the bells.

II.
Hear the mellow wedding bells,
Golden bells!
What a world of happiness their harmony foretells!
Through the balmy air of night
How they **ring** out their delight!
From the molten-golden notes,
And all in tune,
What a liquid ditty floats
To the turtle-dove that listens, while she **gloats**
On the moon!
Oh, from out the sounding cells,
What a **gush** of euphony voluminously wells!
How it swells!
How it dwells
On the Future! how it tells
Of the rapture that impels
To the swinging and the **ringing**
Of the bells, bells, bells,
Of the bells, bells, bells, bells,
Bells, bells, bells—
To the rhyming and the **chiming** of the bells!

III.
Hear the loud alarum bells—
Brazen bells!
What tale of terror, now, their turbulency tells!
In the startled ear of night
How they **scream** out their affright!
Too much horrified to speak,
They can only shriek, **shriek**,
Out of tune,
In a clamorous appealing to the mercy of the fire,
In a mad expostulation with the deaf and frantic fire,
Leaping higher, higher, higher,
With a desperate desire,
And a resolute endeavor
Now—now to sit or never,
By the side of the pale-faced moon.
Oh, the bells, bells, bells!
What a tale their terror tells
Of Despair!
How they **clang**, and **clash**, and **roar**!
What a horror they outpour
On the bosom of the **palpitating** air!
Yet the ear it fully knows,
By the **twanging**,
And the **clanging**,
How the danger ebbs and flows;
Yet the ear distinctly tells,
In the **jangling**,
And the wrangling.
How the danger sinks and swells,
By the sinking or the swelling in the anger of the bells—
Of the bells—
Of the bells, bells, bells, bells,
Bells, bells, bells—
In the clamor and the **clangor** of the bells!

(continue next page)

IV.
Hear the **tolling** of the bells—
Iron bells!
What a world of solemn thought their monody compels!
In the silence of the night,
How we shiver with affright
At the melancholy menace of their tone!
For every sound that floats
From the rust within their throats
Is a **groan**.
And the people—ah, the people—

Mission 12: Onomatopoeia

They that dwell up in the steeple,
All alone,
And who tolling, tolling, tolling,
In that muffled monotone,
Feel a glory in so rolling
On the human heart a stone—
They are neither man nor woman—
They are neither brute nor human—
They are Ghouls:
And their king it is who tolls;
And he rolls, rolls, rolls,
Rolls
A pæan from the bells!
And his merry bosom swells
With the pæan of the bells!
And he dances, and he yells;
Keeping time, time, time,
In a sort of Runic rhyme,
To the pæan of the bells—
Of the bells:
Keeping time, time, time,
In a sort of Runic rhyme,
To the throbbing of the bells—
Of the bells, bells, bells—
To the sobbing of the bells;
Keeping time, time, time,
As he knells, knells, knells,
In a happy Runic rhyme,
To the rolling of the bells—
Of the bells, bells, bells—
To the tolling of the bells,
Of the bells, bells, bells, bells—
Bells, bells, bells—
To the moaning and the groaning of the bells.

## Step 2 Solutions

1. **helicopter**
   lift | whir | takeoff
2. **goose**
   honk | whisper | fly
3. **faucet**
   run | leak | drip
4. **child**
   hiccup | yell | laugh
5. **shoe**
   fit | flashy | squeak
6. **plate**
   clatter | full | stack
7. **leaves**
   change | rustle | bud
8. **bird**
   song | nest | tweet

## Step 3 Solutions

1. The English children's favorite part of the water slide is the splash at the end.
2. Luke loves the clink of dropping coins into his piggy bank.
3. When Kirk watches basketball, he loves hearing the swoosh of the basketball through the net.
4. Ellen loves a horse's neigh when she greets one.
5. The queen doesn't like it when the children mumble.
6. The king loves hearing the sizzle of food in a frying pan.
7. The hose was kinked so the sound of the water coming out was just a dribble.
8. When the king tripped over the hose, the children couldn't help but giggle.

Mission 12: Onomatopoeia

134

# OFFICIAL GUARDIAN MAIL

**Mission 13: British vs. American English Spelling**

Dear guardians,

    Luke submitted a review of a new Happy Holographics game and had his spelling corrected. That isn't so surprising, but our mother had checked his spelling first. It turns out that the company was using British spelling instead of the American spelling that we use.

    We thought it would be important for you to know the differences in spelling. Complete this mission and you'll be able to spell English words two ways and still be correct.

    We are including information from *The Guide to Grammar Galaxy* that you'll need.

Sincerely,

*Kirk, Luke, and Ellen English*
Guardians of Grammar Galaxy

## British vs. American English Spelling

English spelling was inconsistent until the publication of two dictionaries—Johnson's *A Dictionary of the English Language* in 1755 and Webster's *An American Dictionary of the English Language* in 1828.

British English uses more French-dialect spellings of English words. These spelling preferences were generally adopted by former territories of the British Empire. Spelling changes in America and the United Kingdom developed independently. Canadian spelling incorporates both British and American rules. Australia uses less American spelling than Canada but more than New Zealand, which uses British spelling almost exclusively.

**-our/-or**
Unstressed ending syllables are spelled -our in British English and -or in American English.

**-re/-er**
British words ending in -bre or -tre are spelled -ber or -ter in American English.

**-ise/-ize**
British English mostly uses -ise at the end of words while American English uses -ize.

**-ll/-l**
British and American English use a double ll for different words.

**-e**
British English often keeps a silent -e when adding a suffix where American English does not.

A table of some common words spelled differently in British and American English follows.

| British vs. American Spelling of Common Words | | | |
|---|---|---|---|
| British | American | British | American |
| colour | color | neighbour | neighbor |
| centre | center | theatre | theater |
| organise | organize | realise | realize |
| cancelled | canceled | traveller | traveler |
| enrol | enroll | enthral | enthrall |
| ageing | aging | likeable | likable |

Mission 13: British vs. American English Spelling

## ⭐ Step 1: On Guard & Identify British English Words
**On Guard.** *Highlight the correct answer.*

1. Onomatopoeia is a _____ technique.
   satire              literary

2. *Oxymoron* is a _____ word.
   contradictory       science vocabulary

3. *Lev* means _____.
   light               to lift

4. *Inflation* in satire means to make something _____ than it is.
   bigger              smaller

5. Some of Shakespeare's plays are about _____.
   onomatopoeia        mistaken identity


**Say each of these words in a sentence.** *Examples are given.*

| **shamefaced** – embarrassed | I was **shamefaced** when I tripped on the court. |
|---|---|
| **recanted** – took it back | Mother said I was disrespectful, so I **recanted**. |
| **quashed** – suppressed | My father **quashed** a laugh in the serious meeting. |

**Identify British English words.** *Highlight the American English words in this excerpt of Luke's review that should be spelled according to British English rules.* **Hint:** <u>You'll highlight 13 words, some of them repeats.</u>

The first thing I noticed about Happy Holographic's new game, Asteroid Master, is the color of the box. I quickly realized the box wasn't a single color, however. It's holographic and changes color as you turn it.

Happy Holographic knows how to enthrall its gamers. Inside the box, you'll find a sleek game center and a lightweight, virtual-reality headset. There is also a flyer with simple instructions to help you get organized to play.

After I connected the game center and put my headset on, I became a space traveler! I entered a spaceship that took me to an unknown planet for training. The graphics were so clear that I believed I was on the ship!

Upon landing, I was asked to enroll in Masters Academy. The Academy prepares recruits for the asteroid challenges ahead. It's also where I was assigned my dog companion. My dog helper wasn't as cute as my own dog but was thoroughly likable.

I also met the recruits who will be my neighbors in the challenges. Asteroid Master allows you to play with friends or have other players from around the galaxy join your theater for play. I liked that we were supposed to work together to eliminate the asteroids, instead of competing with each other.

Mission 13: British vs. American English Spelling

☆ Step 2: Choose the British Spelling for Each Set of Words

**Using information on British spelling differences, highlight the correct British spelling for each numbered list below.**

1. humor — humour — humer
2. metre — meter — metor
3. recognize — recognice — recognise
4. ageing — aging — age-ing
5. rumer — rumor — rumour
6. sombre — somber — sombur
7. canceled — cancelled — canceld
8. sizeable — sizable — size-able

**Activity.** *Look for British spelling in a BBC news article for kids. See GrammarGalaxyBooks.com/BlueStar for an article.*

Mission 13: British vs. American English Spelling

☆ Step 3: Spell the British English Words Correctly
**Using the excerpt of Luke's review in Step 1, write the correct British spelling in the blanks.** *Note:* Not all words in the blanks need to be spelled differently.

 The first thing I noticed about Happy Holographic's new game, Asteroid Master, is the _____ of the box. I quickly _____ the box wasn't a single _____, however. It's holographic and changes _____ as you turn it.
 Happy Holographic knows how to _____ its gamers. Inside the box, you'll find a sleek game _____ and a lightweight, virtual-reality headset. There is also a _____ with simple instructions to help you get _____ to play.
 After I connected the game _____ and put my headset on, I became a space _____! I entered a spaceship that took me to an unknown planet for training. The graphics were so clear that I believed I was on the ship!
 Upon landing, I was asked to _____ in Masters Academy. The Academy prepares recruits for the asteroid challenges ahead. It's also where I was assigned my dog companion. My dog _____ wasn't as cute as my own dog but was thoroughly _____.
 I also met the recruits who will be my _____ in the challenges. Asteroid Master allows you to play with friends or have other players from around the galaxy join your _____ for play. I liked that we were supposed to work together to _____ the asteroids, instead of competing with each other.


**Vocabulary Victory!** Do you remember what these words mean? *Check Step 1 if you need a reminder.*

| shamefaced | "It's so embarrassing," Luke said, **shamefaced**. |
|---|---|
| recanted | When he saw his wife's expression, he **recanted**. |
| quashed | Luke **quashed** a groan. |

Mission 13: British vs. American English Spelling

## ☆ Advanced Guardians Only
**Write your own video or board game review.** Use as many of the words in the British-spelling word box as you can.

| humour    | colour      | neighbour | calibre |
| centre    | meagre      | defence   | offence |
| recognise | quarrelling | likeable  | grey    |
| cosy      | chequer     |           |         |

_____
_____
_____
_____
_____
_____
_____
_____
_____
_____
_____
_____
_____
_____
_____
_____
_____
_____
_____
_____
_____
_____
_____
_____
_____

# OFFICIAL GUARDIAN MAIL

**Mission 13: Update**

Dear guardian friends,

Thank you for helping Luke make the needed spelling changes in his review. Happy Holographics was very happy with it!

Whether you use more British or American English spellings, we hope you learned something. By the way, we enjoyed reading your reviews and plan to play some of your top-rated games soon.

We are including the solutions to your mission for you to review.

Sincerely,

*Kirk, Luke, and Ellen English*
Guardians of Grammar Galaxy

Mission 13: British vs. American English Spelling

Step 1 Solutions

**On Guard.**

1. Onomatopoeia is a _____ technique.
   satire          literary

2. Oxymoron is a _____ word.
   contradictory          science vocabulary

3. Lev means _____.
   light          to lift

4. Inflation in satire means to make something _____ than it is.
   bigger          smaller

5. Some of Shakespeare's plays are about _____.
   onomatopoeia          mistaken identity

**Highlight British English words.**

    The first thing I noticed about Happy Holographic's new game, Asteroid Master, is the color of the box. I quickly realized the box wasn't a single color, however. It's holographic and changes color as you turn it.
    Happy Holographic knows how to enthrall its gamers. Inside the box, you'll find a sleek game center and a lightweight, virtual-reality headset. There is also a flyer with simple instructions to help you get organized to play.
    After I connected the game center and put my headset on, I became a space traveler! I entered a spaceship that took me to an unknown planet for training. The graphics were so clear that I believed I was on the ship!
    Upon landing, I was asked to enroll in Masters Academy. The Academy prepares recruits for the asteroid challenges ahead. It's also where I was assigned my dog companion. My dog helper wasn't as cute as my own dog but was thoroughly likable.
    I also met the recruits who will be my neighbors in the challenges. Asteroid Master allows you to play with friends or have other players from around the galaxy join your theater for play. I liked that we were supposed to work together to eliminate the asteroids, instead of competing with each other.

Step 2 Solutions

| | | | |
|---|---|---|---|
| 1. | humor | humour | humer |
| 2. | metre | meter | metor |
| 3. | recognize | recognice | recognise |
| 4. | ageing | aging | age-ing |
| 5. | rumer | rumor | rumour |
| 6. | sombre | somber | sombur |
| 7. | canceled | cancelled | canceld |
| 8. | sizeable | sizable | size-able |

Step 3 Solutions

    The first thing I noticed about Happy Holographic's new game, Asteroid Master, is the colour of the box. I quickly realised the box wasn't a single colour, however. It's holographic and changes colour as you turn it.
    Happy Holographic knows how to enthral its gamers. Inside the box, you'll find a sleek game centre and a lightweight, virtual-reality headset. There is also a flyer with simple instructions to help you get organised to play.
    After I connected the game centre and put my headset on, I became a space traveller! I entered a spaceship that took me to an unknown planet for training. The graphics were so clear that I believed I was on the ship!
    Upon landing, I was asked to enrol in Masters Academy. The Academy prepares recruits for the asteroid challenges ahead. It's also where I was assigned my dog companion. My dog helper wasn't as cute as my own dog but was thoroughly likeable.
    I also met the recruits who will be my neighbors in the challenges. Asteroid Master allows you to play with friends or have other players from around the galaxy join your theatre for play. I liked that we were supposed to work together to eliminate the asteroids, instead of competing with each other.

# OFFICIAL GUARDIAN MAIL

**Mission 14: British Vocabulary**

Hey there mates,

We have another mission for you while Luke is visiting the Happy Holographics campus in Manchester. There are some differences in British and American English vocabulary that can cause confusion. Luke has experienced this confusion, thinking his driver was going to put his luggage inside a boot—the kind you wear on your foot!

We are including a chart with some common vocabulary differences that you will need for this mission. By the way, *mate* is a British word for friend. Thank you in advance for being our friends and doing your best on this mission.

Sincerely,

*Kirk and Ellen English*
Guardians of Grammar Galaxy

| American | British |
|---|---|
| attorney | barrister, solicitor |
| cookie | biscuit |
| trunk | boot |
| drug store | chemist's |
| french fries | chips |
| stove | cooker |
| crib | cot |
| pacifier | dummy |
| jumper | sweater |
| garbage collector | dustman |
| generator | dynamo |
| overpass | flyover |
| billboard | hoarding |
| vacation | holiday |
| elevator | lift |
| truck | lorry |
| diaper | nappy |
| nursing home | private hospital |
| sidewalk | pavement |
| gasoline | petrol |
| mailbox | postbox |
| potato chips | crisps |
| stroller | push-chair |
| line | queue |
| can | tin |
| flashlight | torch |

Mission 14: British Vocabulary

⭐ Step 1: On Guard & Find the British Vocabulary
**On Guard.** *Highlight the correct answer.*

1. The British spelling is:
   color        colour        collar

2. An onomatopoeia word is:
   slam         shout         clang

3. An oxymoron example is:
   old soul     found missing     small group

4. A word root that means movement is:
   kinesis      dyna          syn

5. A cartoon drawing of a politician with a large head is an example of:
   oxymoron     onomatopoeia     satire


**Say each of these words in a sentence.** *Examples are given.*

| **requisite** – necessary | My mother says cleaning my room is **requisite** for having a snack. |
|---|---|
| **sentiment** – feeling | Dad says laws shouldn't be based on **sentiment**. |
| **sublime** – magnificent | The views from our mountain cabin are **sublime**. |

Mission 14: British Vocabulary

**Find the British vocabulary**. *Highlight every British vocabulary word you find in the sentences below.* **Note:** *Use the vocabulary chart we sent you*.

1. "I'll just put your luggage in the boot."

2. "Are you on holiday?"

3. "I like your jumper."

4. "I can't see around this lorry."

5. "Would you mind if I stopped at the chemist's shop on the way?"

6. "I had to get some nappies and a new dummy for the wife, too."

7. "We have to begin by having you meet with our barrister."

8. "Would you like a biscuit while you wait?"

Mission 14: British Vocabulary

⭐ Step 2: Highlight the British Vocabulary Word That Belongs in the Blank
**Choose the British vocabulary word that makes sense in each sentence and highlight it.**

1. Cook just put a pot of soup on the _____.
   stove            cooker            fireplace

2. The queen just gave away the _____ we used as babies.
   cot              crib              bed

3. The king has a _____ to use in case the castle loses power.
   generator        dynamo            furnace

4. Aunt Iseen is superstitious about traveling under a/an _____.
   dynamo           flyover           overpass

5. The castle has a/an _____ between floors that is rarely used.
   elevator         chute             lift

6. Cook prefers not to use vegetables that come in a _____.
   box              can               tin

7. When Luke was little, the queen took him for walks in a _____.
   push-chair       stroller          carriage

8. The king hates going anywhere where he has to stand in a _____.
   line             row               queue

**Activity.** *Use as many British vocabulary words (or American if you use British English) as possible while playing a game. Does anyone notice?*

Mission 14: British Vocabulary

⭐ Step 3: Write the American English Word
**For each British vocabulary word you highlighted in step 1, write the American vocabulary word on the line below each sentence.** *Note:* <u>Some sentences may have more than one word.</u>

1. "I'll just put your luggage in the boot."

   _____

2. "Are you on holiday?"

   _____

3. "I like your jumper."

   _____

4. "I can't see around this lorry."

   _____

5. "Would you mind if I stopped at the chemist's shop on the way?"

   _____

6. "I had to get some nappies and a new dummy for the wife, too."

   _____

7. "We have to begin by having you meet with our barrister."

   _____

8. "Would you like a biscuit while you wait?"

   _____

Mission 14: British Vocabulary

**Vocabulary Victory!** Do you remember what these words mean? *Check Step 1 if you need a reminder.*

| requisite | Their presence wouldn't be **requisite**. |
|---|---|
| sentiment | The king wanted to continue the positive **sentiment**. |
| sublime | "That will be **sublime**," Luke answered. |

☆ <u>Advanced Guardians Only</u>
**Write a description of what your visiting guests could expect, using as many British or American vocabulary words (whichever you use less often) as possible.** *Use the list of vocabulary words we provided you for inspiration.*

_____
_____
_____
_____
_____
_____
_____
_____
_____
_____
_____
_____
_____
_____
_____
_____
_____
_____
_____
_____

Mission 14: British Vocabulary

# OFFICIAL GUARDIAN MAIL

**Mission 14: Update**

Dear mates,

   I (Luke) was so confused by the vocabulary when I arrived in Manchester. But after learning the meaning of the words, I was chuffed. That means I was pleased or delighted. I hope you found this mission as much fun as I did.

   The three of us enjoyed your descriptions of what a visit would be like. We know you did a proper job on your mission (that means you did well), but we are sending the solutions for you to review anyway.

Sincerely,

*Kirk, Luke, and Ellen English*
Guardians of Grammar Galaxy

Mission 14: British Vocabulary

Step 1 Solutions

**On Guard**.

1. The British spelling is:
   color              **colour**              collar
2. An onomatopoeia word is:
   slam              shout              **clang**
3. An oxymoron example is:
   old soul              **found missing**              small group
4. A word root that means movement is:
   **kinesis**              dyna              syn
5. A cartoon drawing of a politician with a large head is an example of:
   oxymoron              onomatopoeia              **satire**

**Find the British vocabulary.**

1. "I'll just put your luggage in the **boot**."
2. "Are you on **holiday**?"
3. "I like your **jumper**."
4. "I can't see around this **lorry**."
5. "Would you mind if I stopped at the **chemist's** shop on the way?"
6. "I had to get some **nappies** and a new **dummy** for the wife, too."
7. "We have to begin by having you meet with our **barrister**."
8. "Would you like a **biscuit** while you wait?"

Step 2 Solutions

1. Cook just put a pot of soup on the _____.
   stove              **cooker**              fireplace
2. The queen just gave away the _____ we used as babies.
   **cot**              crib              bed
3. The king has a _____ to use in case the castle loses power.
   generator              **dynamo**              furnace
4. Aunt Iseen is superstitious about traveling under a/an _____.
   dynamo              **flyover**              overpass
5. The castle has a/an _____ between floors that is rarely used.
   elevator              chute              **lift**
6. Cook prefers not to use vegetables that come in a _____.
   box              can              **tin**
7. When Luke was little, the queen took him for walks in a _____.
   **push-chair**              stroller              carriage
8. The king hates going anywhere where he has to stand in a _____.
   line              row              **queue**

Step 3 Solutions

1. "I'll just put your luggage in the boot."
trunk
2. "Are you on holiday?"
vacation
3. "I like your jumper."
sweater
4. "I can't see around this lorry."
truck
5. "Would you mind if I stopped at the chemist's shop on the way?"
drug store
6. "I had to get some nappies and a new dummy for the wife, too."
diapers, pacifier
7. "We have to begin by having you meet with our barrister."
attorney
8. "Would you like a biscuit while you wait?"
cookie

**Mission 15: Confused Vocabulary Words**

Dear guardians,

Have your parents been worried about you using the wrong vocabulary words like *supposably* when you mean *supposedly*? We know why! There is a masquerade ball on planet Vocabulary that has words being mistaken for one another.

We are on our way to the planet, but we need your help. Please choose the correct vocabulary words in this mission so we can tell these words apart. Thank you in advance for completing this mission as soon as possible.

We are including information from *The Guide to Grammar Galaxy* to help you.

Sincerely,

*Kirk, Luke, and Ellen English*
Guardians of Grammar Galaxy

Mission 15: Confused Vocabulary Words

| Commonly Confused Vocabulary Words | | | | | |
|---|---|---|---|---|---|
| Word | Part of Speech; Meaning | Word | Part of Speech; Meaning | Word | Part of Speech; Meaning |
| a lot | **Article, Noun**; many | alot | misspelling | allot | **Verb**; give as share; set apart |
| awhile | **Adv.**; done a short time | a while | **Noun**; period of time | | |
| among | **Prep.**; amid 3 or more items not specified | between | **Prep.**; in the middle of 2 or more specific items | | |
| assure | **Verb**; tell to remove doubt | ensure | **Verb**; make certain | insure | **Verb**; provide security for |
| capital | **Noun**; city seat of government | capitol | **Noun**; legislative building | | |
| complement | **Noun**; thing that completes **Verb**; make perfect | compliment | **Noun**; expression of praise **Verb**; commend | | |
| emigrate | **Verb**; leave country to live elsewhere | immigrate | **Verb**; come to country to live | | |
| historic | **Adj.**; important in history | historical | **Adj.**; about the past | | |
| i.e. | **Abbrev.**; in other words | e.g. | **Abbrev.**; for example | | |
| into | **Prep.**; indicates where | in to | **Adv., Prep.**; indicates purpose | | |
| less | **Adj.**; used with uncountable nouns | fewer | **Adj.**; used with countable nouns | | |
| login | **Noun**; process to gain computer access | log in | **Verb, Prep.**; start a computer or system session | | |
| principal | **Noun**; school director | principle | **Noun**; value | | |
| stationary | **Adj.**; immovable | stationery | **Noun**; printed paper | | |
| supposably | **Adv.**; may be conceived or imagined | supposedly | **Adv.**; truth is doubtful | | |

Abbrev.= abbreviation; Adj.= adjective; Adv.= adverb; Prep.=preposition

Mission 15: Confused Vocabulary Words

## ☆ Step 1: On Guard & Identify Word Meaning

**On Guard.** *Use a highlighter to mark TRUE or FALSE for each question.*

1. The British English word for cookie is *crisp*.                TRUE   FALSE

2. *Realise* is the British English spelling.                     TRUE   FALSE

3. Air sounds are one of the five types of onomatopoeia.          TRUE   FALSE

4. *Freezer burn* is an oxymoron we don't notice much.            TRUE   FALSE

5. The word root *bene* means to move away.                       TRUE   FALSE


**Say each of these words in a sentence.** *Examples are given.*

| **judiciously** – carefully | Grandma listened to both sides of the argument **judiciously**. |
|---|---|
| **impertinent** – disrespectful | My dad's boss doesn't tolerate **impertinent** remarks. |
| **differentiated** – separated | My friends are identical twins and their appearance can't be **differentiated**. |

**Identify word meaning.** *The underlined vocabulary word in each sentence is used <u>correctly</u>. Highlight the meaning of the word from the choices below the sentence.* **Hint:** <u>Use the chart we sent you.</u>

1. Father likes to say it was a <u>historic</u> day when he met Mother.
   important in history        about the past

2. The queen uses floral <u>stationery</u> for her correspondence.
   immovable        printed paper

3. Integrity is a <u>principle</u> the king and queen hold dear.
   value        school director

4. Father wants to <u>ensure</u> that children keep reading.
   make certain        provide security for

5. The king is reluctant to <u>allot</u> part of his flower garden for vegetables.
   many        give as share

6. The king tells Ellen she is a rose <u>among</u> thorns.
   amid 3+ unspecified        in the middle of 2+ specific

7. Even now, the king gets nervous when walking into the <u>capitol</u> building.
   legislative building        city seat of government

8. The king sometimes forgets to <u>compliment</u> the queen.
   expression of praise        make perfect

Mission 15: Confused Vocabulary Words

⭐ Step 2: Choose the Correct Vocabulary Word
**Highlight the word that belongs in the blank for each sentence.** *Hint: Use the part of speech of the word in parentheses when given and the chart we sent.*

1. Kirk has been working on a spaceship model _____ (adverb).
   awhile          a while

2. He enjoys going _____ (preposition) the studio to work alone.
   into            in to

3. His first step is to _____ (verb; preposition) to the computer to view the instructions.
   login           log in

4. He wants to _____ that he puts the model together correctly.
   assure          ensure          insure

5. He has enjoyed working on an older, _____ spaceship model.
   historic        historical

6. However, he has had to spend more time on some pieces (____, photo etch accessories, decals, and lighting).
   i.e.            e.g.

7. He has sometimes made a mistake choosing _____ two decals.
   between         among

8. But Kirk has far _____ pieces left to put in place than when he started.
   less            fewer


**Activity.** Work on a puzzle or model of your choice that has <u>a lot</u> of pieces. Work on it for <u>a while</u>. Keep it <u>stationary</u>. <u>Log in</u> to a website to <u>ensure</u> that you are following directions or creating the right picture. Work until you have <u>fewer</u> pieces left than when you started. Make sure you <u>compliment</u> yourself for a job well done.

159

Mission 15: Confused Vocabulary Words

⭐ Step 3: Write the Correct Vocabulary Word in the Blank
**Write the word from the vocabulary chart that belongs in the sentence.**
*Choose the word that makes the most sense.*

1. _____ the Gremlin won't be causing more problems.

2. Parliament thinks they have him under control (_____, they have passed some laws).

3. They believe the Gremlin will _____ to another galaxy.

4. Parliament wants to _____ us that the galaxy is safe.

5. It has been _____ since the Gremlin has caused a crisis.

6. But having _____ crises does not mean the Gremlin is under control.

7. There is agreement _____ Parliament members that we don't need to worry about the Gremlin.

8. The king plans to speak to Parliament in the _____ building to change their minds.


**Vocabulary Victory!** Do you remember what these words mean? *Check Step 1 if you need a reminder.*

| judiciously | "But if you keep writing this way, you won't know proper vocabulary when you are writing a formal paper," the queen said **judiciously**. |
|---|---|
| apprised | That's no excuse for being **impertinent** with your Mother. |
| differentiated | Confused vocabulary words can be **differentiated** by their part of speech. |

Mission 15: Confused Vocabulary Words

## ⭐ Advanced Guardians Only

**Write your opinion about a house rule or another rule or law.** Don't be impertinent! But use at least five of this mission's vocabulary words correctly in your writing. Highlight the words. Type or write on the lines below.

Mission 15: Confused Vocabulary Words

**Mission 15: Update**

Dear guardian friends,

    We want to assure you that the vocabulary confusion should be coming to an end. With your help, we were able to differentiate confused words at the masquerade ball. Father was able to keep new words from going into the ball. That seemed to kill the energy, and the words started leaving.

    But we might have missed some words in costume. Keep an eye out for more confused vocabulary words. And be sure to check the solutions to this mission.

    Thank you for keeping the galaxy strong!

Sincerely,

*Kirk, Luke, and Ellen English*
Guardians of Grammar Galaxy

Mission 15: Confused Vocabulary

Step 1 Solutions
**On Guard.**

1. The British English word for cookie is *crisp*. — TRUE **FALSE**
2. *Realise* is the British English spelling. — **TRUE** FALSE
3. Air sounds are one of the five types of onomatopoeia. — **TRUE** FALSE
4. *Freezer burn* is an oxymoron we don't notice much. — **TRUE** FALSE
5. The word root *bene* means to move away. — TRUE **FALSE**

**Identify word meaning.**

1. Father likes to say it was a <u>historic</u> day when he met Mother.
   **important in history**   about the past
2. The queen uses floral <u>stationery</u> for her correspondence.
   immovable   **printed paper**
3. Integrity is a <u>principle</u> the king and queen hold dear.
   **value**   school director
4. Father wants to <u>ensure</u> that children keep reading.
   **make certain**   provide security for
5. The king is reluctant to <u>allot</u> part of his flower garden for vegetables.
   many   **give as share**
6. The king tells Ellen she is a rose <u>among</u> thorns.
   **amid 3+ unspecified**   in the middle of 2+ specific
7. Even now, the king gets nervous when walking into the <u>capitol</u> building.
   **legislative building**   city seat of government
8. The king sometimes forgets to <u>compliment</u> the queen.
   **expression of praise**   make perfect

Step 2 Solutions

1. Kirk has been working on a spaceship model _____ (adverb).
   **awhile**   a while
2. He enjoys going _____ (preposition) the studio to work alone.
   **into**   in to
3. His first step is to _____ (verb; preposition) to the computer to view the instructions.
   login   **log in**
4. He wants to _____ that he puts the model together correctly.
   assure   **ensure**   insure
5. He has enjoyed working on an older, _____ spaceship model.
   historic   **historical**
6. However, he has had to spend more time on some pieces (____, photo etch accessories, decals, and lighting).
   i.e.   **e.g.**
7. He has sometimes made a mistake choosing _____ two decals.
   **between**   among
8. But Kirk has far _____ pieces left to put in place than when he started.
   less   **fewer**

Step 3 Solutions

1. <u>Supposedly</u> the Gremlin won't be causing more problems.
2. Parliament thinks they have him under control (<u>i.e.,</u> they have passed some laws).
3. They believe the Gremlin will <u>emigrate</u> to another galaxy.
4. Parliament wants to <u>assure</u> us that the galaxy is safe.
5. It has been <u>a while</u> since the Gremlin has caused a crisis.
6. But having <u>fewer</u> crises does not mean the Gremlin is under control.
7. There is agreement <u>among</u> Parliament members that we don't need to worry about the Gremlin.
8. The king plans to speak to Parliament in the <u>capitol</u> building to change their minds.

**Mission 16: Vocabulary Mnemonics**

Dear guardians,

We are exuberant about this mission! If you don't remember what *exuberant* means, don't worry. You'll learn ways to remember vocabulary words like it in this mission. For example, you can imagine an **ex-Uber** driver who is enthusiastic about starting an **ant** farm. Now you'll remember than exuberant means enthusiastic.

Start your mission to practice even more memory tricks.

Sincerely,
*Kirk and Ellen English*
Guardians of Grammar Galaxy

☆ Step 1: On Guard & Study the Mnemonic Cartoons
**On Guard.** *Highlight the correct answer for each statement.*

1. The word or phrase meaning *many* is:
   allot          alot          a lot

2. The British English word for billboard is:
   dynamo          hoarding          solicitor

3. The correct British English spelling is:
   traveller          traveler          travelour

4. An onomatopoeia word is:
   dish          wish          swish

5. The following is an oxymoron:
   large statue          small fortune          kitchen sink


**Say each of these words in a sentence.** *Examples are given.*

| | |
|---|---|
| **scurried** – hurried | My mom screamed when the mice **scurried** behind the couch. |
| **quandary** – dilemma | Choosing which candy to get is always a **quandary** for me. |
| **composed** – unemotional | My grandma was not **composed** when my baby sister was born. |

Mission 16: Vocabulary Mnemonics

**Study the mnemonic cartoons.** *Then highlight the correct meaning for each vocabulary word on the next page, without using a dictionary.*

1. **largesse** means:
   lack of respect　　　roomy　　　generous with gifts

2. **winsome** means:
   appealing　　　brief　　　generous with gifts

3. **truculent** means:
   play excitedly　　　roomy　　　quick to fight

4. **lachrymose** means:
   play excitedly　　　brief　　　tearful

5. **cavort** means:
   play excitedly　　　roomy　　　quick to fight

6. **capacious** means:
   Appealing　　　roomy　　　tearful

## ⭐ Step 2: Determine Vocabulary Meaning from Lyrics

**Look at the underlined word in each song lyric.** *Using the lyrics as context, highlight the meaning of the word on the right without using a dictionary.*

| | |
|---|---|
| Be our guest<br>Beef ragout<br>Cheese souffle<br>Pie and pudding "en flambe"<br>We'll prepare and serve with flair<br>A <u>culinary</u> cabaret<br>-"Be Our Guest" by Howard Ashman | serving<br>dancing<br>cooking |
| The snow glows white on the mountain tonight<br>Not a footprint to be seen<br>A kingdom of <u>isolation</u><br>And it looks like I'm the queen<br>-"Let It Go" by Idina Menzel | loneliness<br>royalty<br>cold |
| I worked in the colony, paying my dues<br>Accepting without question the <u>prevailing</u> views<br>That a young man's life was one long grind<br>Diggin' holes, standin' guard till it crossed my mind<br>-"Hakuna Matata" by Jimmy Cliff, Lebo M. | royal<br>dominant<br>animal |
| Well you can knock me down<br>Laugh in my face<br><u>Slander</u> my name all over the place<br>Do anything that you want to do<br>But uh uh honey<br>Lay off my blue suede shoes<br>-"Blue Suede Shoes" by Carl Perkins | say<br>mispronounce<br>insult |
| And up in the nursery an <u>absurd</u> little bird<br>Is popping out to say "cuckoo"<br>Cuckoo, cuckoo<br>-"So Long, Farewell" by Oscar Hammerstein II | small<br>ridiculous<br>big |

**Activity.** With your teacher's guidance, look up song lyrics to help you remember the meaning of new vocabulary words. Or, listen to these songs to help you remember the meaning of the words below. See GrammarGalaxyBooks.com/BlueStar for links.

destiny (future) – "You've Got a Friend in Me"
optic (visual) – "If I Didn't Have You"
crustacean (shellfish) – "Kiss the Girl"

Mission 16: Vocabulary Mnemonics

☆ Step 3: Write a Mnemonic Saying

**For each vocabulary word, complete the saying to help you remember its meaning.** Use a word from the word box that makes sense and includes part of the vocabulary word.

| grandstand | probation | despises | punctuation |
| con | pupils | villain | morph |
| rage | village | aggravated | appropriate |

1. **punctilious (detail oriented)**
My grammar teacher is punctilious about _____.

2. **umbrage (anger at being offended)**
My friend took umbrage at my joke and flew into a _____.

3. **vilify (spread negative information about)**
Dad says we shouldn't vilify someone if we don't know that they're the _____.

4. **aggrandize (make something bigger or more important)**
The politician tends to aggrandize in the _____.

5. **amorphous (shapeless)**
In the potter's hand, the amorphous clay will _____ into something beautiful.

6. **approbation (approval)**
The approbation was that the juvenile offender should be given _____.

7. **connived (schemed)**
The _____ artist connived a way to get the woman's money.

8. **despot (dictator)**
The despot _____ the poor people in his country.

170

**Vocabulary Victory!** Do you remember what these words mean? *Check Step 1 if you need a reminder.*

| scurried | He grabbed the bag of trash and **scurried** out the door with it. |
|---|---|
| quandary | He had a **quandary** important enough to interrupt her. |
| composed | Despite his intention to be **composed**, he couldn't hold back the tears. |

Mission 16: Vocabulary Mnemonics

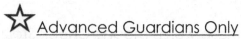 Advanced Guardians Only
**Create cartoon mnemonics for the two vocabulary words below.** *You may draw them, print and paste graphics, or create them using a graphic program. Be sure to include the word on your card.* **Hint:** *Look up the word in a mnemonic dictionary if you need ideas. Find links at GrammarGalaxyBooks.com/BlueStar.*

1. **abstemious** – eats and drinks sparingly

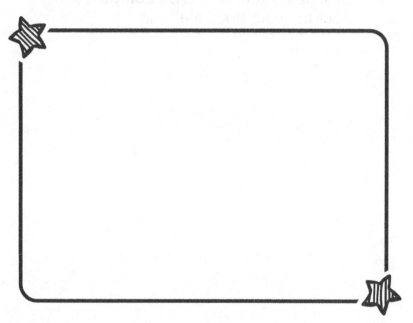

2. **nebulous** – lacking definite form

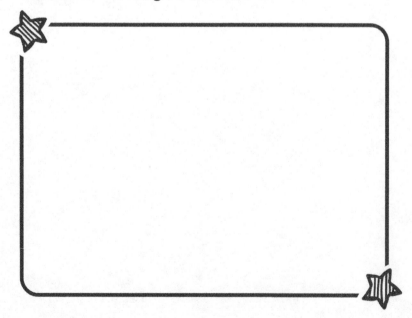

**Mission 16: Update**

Dear conscientious (reliable) guardians,

We hope you are remembering more vocabulary than ever after using mnemonics. We love the cartoons you came up with. Luke is going to use mnemonics to help him remember the British vocabulary he learned. That might help you, too.

We are including the solutions to this mission. Please check them scrupulously (carefully).

Sincerely,

*Kirk, Luke, and Ellen English*
Guardians of Grammar Galaxy

## Step 1 Solutions

**On Guard.**

1. The word or phrase meaning *many* is:
    allot     alot     **a lot**
2. The British English word for billboard is:
    dynamo     **hoarding**     solicitor
3. The correct British English spelling is:
    **traveller**     traveler     travelour
4. An onomatopoeia word is:
    dish     wish     **swish**
5. The following is an oxymoron:
    large statue     **small fortune**     kitchen sink

**Study the mnemonic cartoons.**

1. **largesse** means:
    lack of respect     roomy     **generous with gifts**
2. **winsome** means:
    **appealing**     brief     generous with gifts
3. **truculent** means:
    play excitedly     roomy     **quick to fight**
4. **lachrymose** means:
    play excitedly     brief     **tearful**
5. **cavort** means:
    **play excitedly**     roomy     quick to fight
6. **capacious** means:
    appealing     **roomy**     tearful

## Step 2 Solutions

| | |
|---|---|
| Be our guest<br>Beef ragout<br>Cheese souffle<br>Pie and pudding "en flambe"<br>We'll prepare and serve with flair<br>A <u>culinary</u> cabaret<br>-"Be Our Guest" by Howard Ashman | serving<br>dancing<br>**cooking** |
| The snow glows white on the mountain tonight<br>Not a footprint to be seen<br>A kingdom of <u>isolation</u><br>And it looks like I'm the queen<br>-"Let It Go" by Idina Menzel | **loneliness**<br>royalty<br>cold |
| I worked in the colony, paying my dues<br>Accepting without question the <u>prevailing</u> views<br>That a young man's life was one long grind<br>Diggin' holes, standin' guard till it crossed my mind<br>-"Hakuna Matata" by Jimmy Cliff, Lebo M. | royal<br>**dominant**<br>animal |
| Well you can knock me down<br>Laugh in my face<br><u>Slander</u> my name all over the place<br>Do anything that you want to do<br>But uh uh honey<br>Lay off my blue suede shoes<br>-"Blue Suede Shoes" by Carl Perkins | say<br>mispronounce<br>**insult** |
| And up in the nursery an <u>absurd</u> little bird<br>Is popping out to say "cuckoo"<br>Cuckoo, cuckoo<br>-"So Long, Farewell" by Oscar Hammerstein II | small<br>**ridiculous**<br>big |

## Step 3 Solutions

**1. punctilious (detail oriented)**
My grammar teacher is punctilious about <u>punctuation</u>.
**2. umbrage (anger at being offended)**
My friend took umbrage at my joke and flew into a <u>rage</u>.

Mission 16: Vocabulary Mnemonics

3. **vilify (spread negative information about)**
Dad says we shouldn't vilify someone if we don't know that they're the <u>villain</u>.

4. **aggrandize (make something bigger or more important)**
The politician tends to aggrandize in the <u>grandstand</u>.

5. **amorphous (shapeless)**
In the potter's hand, the amorphous clay will <u>morph</u> into something beautiful.

6. **approbation (approval)**
The approbation was that the juvenile offender should be given <u>probation</u>.

7. **connived (schemed)**
The <u>con</u> artist connived a way to get the woman's money.

8. **despot (dictator)**
The despot <u>despises</u> the poor people in his country.

**Advanced Guardians.** Answers will vary.

Abstemious may depict a bodybuilder with obvious abdominal muscles. Nebulous may depict a nebula in space.

Mission 16: Vocabulary Mnemonics

**Mission 17: Prefixes, Suffixes, and Root Words**

Attention guardians:

This is your king here. Kirk, Luke, Ellen, and the queen are at the new Action Theme Park on planet Vocabulary. If you were planning a trip, don't bother. The place isn't as advertised. It's a waste of money! But that's not why I'm writing.

Action Theme Park has a number of prefixes, suffixes, and root words working there. That means that adults and stud—s can't use them here on planet English. My family made a list of these word parts. You'll recognize some of them from your science vocabulary mission. I am including the list with more information you need to complete this mission.

Thank you in advance for your service in getting these word parts back to their real jobs.

Sincerely,
*His Royal Highness*
King of Grammar Galaxy

P.S. I am taking steps to have Action Theme Park shut down.

| Prefixes, Root Words, Suffixes | | |
|---|---|---|
| **Prefixes** | **Definition** | **Example** |
| il-, im-, in-, ir- | not | illegal, immature, innate, irrational |
| inter- | between | interstate |
| micro- | small | microscopic |
| super- | above/on top of | superior |
| trans- | across/through/change | transport, transform |
| uni- | one | unicycle |
| **Root Words** | **Definition** | **Example** |
| bene | good | beneficial |
| chron | time | chronological |
| hydr | water | hydration |
| port | carry | portable |
| scrib, script | write | manuscript |
| spect | see, observe | inspect |
| therm | heat | thermometer |
| vac | empty | vacuum |
| **Suffixes** | **Definition** | **Example** |
| -age | result of action, collection | drainage |
| -ant, -ent | action, condition or causing | contestant, obedient |
| -eous, -ious, -ous | full of, characterized by | nauseous, insidious, jealous |
| -ic | related to, characterized by | historic |
| -ity, -ty | state or quality of | honesty |
| -ize | make, cause to become | apologize |

Mission 17: Prefixes, Suffixes & Root Words

## ⭐ Step 1: On Guard & Identify the Correct Word Part

**On Guard.** *Answer the questions or answer them verbally for your teacher.*

1. What is a mnemonic?

2. What is one way that confused vocabulary words can be differentiated?

3. Why are there differences in British and American vocabulary?

4. What is one type of onomatopoeia sound?

5. What is an oxymoron?

**Say each of these words in a sentence.** *Examples are given.*

| | |
|---|---|
| **profusely** – abundantly | Dad thanked me **profusely** for helping with yard work. |
| **steep** – expensive | Dad said we could ski if the pass prices weren't so **steep**. |
| **cynically** – skeptically | My brother approaches every movie remake **cynically**. |

# Mission 17: Prefixes, Suffixes & Root Words

**Identify the correct word part.** *For each line in the sentences below, highlight the prefix, suffix, or root word that makes the most sense in the blank.* **Hint:** <u>Use the list I sent and the dictionary if you need help</u>.

1. The king's football team was winning until the quarterback threw an _____ception.

    in                  inter             super

2. The king wanted to save money, but the queen wanted to host an eleg_____ affair.

    in                  ous             ant

3. The queen convinced the king to spend the money because the event would _____fit the poor.

    bene            trans           scrib

4. The queen thought the event would be adventur_____.

    ic                  ous             ity

5. The king thought the event would be too much to man_____.

    eous            ize             age

6. The queen thought a masquerade ball would be myster_____.

    eous            ious            ous

7. She wanted the guards dressed in _____form.

    uni                 super           micro

8. The king tried not to be _____patient with her ideas.

    in                  il                 im

Mission 17: Prefixes, Suffixes & Root Words

⭐ Step 2: Guess the Vocabulary Word Meaning
**Highlight the most likely meaning of the vocabulary word.** *Use the list provided, but don't use a dictionary.*

1. **interloper**
   cyclist            traveler                    intruder

2. **imperceptible**
   uncatchable        impossible to perceive      not perfect

3. **transcutaneous**
   across skin        between cuts                above skin

4. **superscript**
   small words        writing that's above        one letter

5. **bounteous**
   see clearly        to make more                full of bounty

6. **ubiquity**
   make present       quality of being everywhere causing to quit

7. **portage**
   shipping fee       carrying of boat or cargo   observing a port

8. **synchronize**
   timeless           not at same time            causing at same time


**Activity.** See how many words you and a partner (teacher, sibling, friend) can think of that start with the following prefixes. Each of you put a hash mark for every <u>unique</u> word you say out loud in the columns below. Who can think of the most words? Only use a dictionary to verify a word.

| im- | | |
|---|---|---|
| inter- | | |
| micro- | | |
| super- | | |
| trans- | | |
| uni- | | |

Mission 17: Prefixes, Suffixes & Root Words

⭐ Step 3: Write the Correct Word Part
**Write the prefix, suffix, or root word that makes the most sense in the blank.**
*Review the story and the word chart for help.*

1. The king wondered if the park had an electrical out_____.

2. He expected that the park would apolog_____ for closing early.

3. He found the whole thing very myster_____.

4. The king promised he would deal with the park's dishones_____.

5. The king thought that his sending out the mission made Kirk nerv_____.

6. Ellen thought the Chrono _____port would take them to a different time, but it was just a simple tram.

7. She was disappointed that she lost at _____ Balloon Darts, in which she tried to aim between the balloons.

8. Luke was also disappointed that he didn't get to ride high above the park on the _____sonic roller coaster.

**Vocabulary Victory!** Do you remember what these words mean? *Check Step 1 if you need a reminder.*

| profusely | Kirk, Luke, and Ellen thanked her **profusely** for taking them |
| steep | Her eyes widened in surprise at the **steep** price. |
| cynically | "Those things are always a ripoff," Luke said **cynically**. |

Mission 17: Prefixes, Suffixes & Root Words

☆ Advanced Guardians Only
**Write a letter to the prefixes, suffixes, and root words working at Action Theme Park.** *Share the words they are in that are most important to your life. Convince them that their work in the English language is more important than their work in a theme park. Be sure to sign it!*

Dear word parts at Action Theme Park,
    I am writing to encourage you to quit your job. Here's why.

_____
_____
_____
_____
_____
_____
_____
_____
_____
_____
_____
_____
_____
_____
_____
_____
_____
_____
_____
_____
_____
_____

Sincerely,


Guardian of the Galaxy

# OFFICIAL GUARDIAN MAIL

**Mission 17: Update**

Dear guardians,

    Were you surprised to get a mission direct from the king? We were certainly surprised by what we experienced at Action Theme Park. But we have good news! The park is closed. We gave your excellent letters to the word parts. We had to be sneaky getting them handed out. But so many word parts quit their jobs that the park closed, even before our father took legal action. Well done, friends.

    We hope you will remember the meaning of these word parts because, as you now know, we use them a lot. We are sending you the solutions to your mission.

With gratitude,

*Kirk, Luke, and Ellen English*
Guardians of Grammar Galaxy

Mission 17: Prefixes, Suffixes & Root Words

Step 1 Solutions
**On Guard.**
1. What is a mnemonic?
   **A memory aid.**
2. What is one way that confused vocabulary words can be differentiated?
   **By their part of speech, unique spelling, or specific meaning.**
3. Why are there differences in British and American vocabulary?
   **People lived apart and developed unique word meanings.**
4. What is one type of onomatopoeia sound?
   **Collision, animal, vocal, water, air**
5. What is an oxymoron?
   **A figure of speech that is a combination of literal opposites**

**Identify the correct word part.**
1. The king's football team was winning until the quarterback threw an _____ception.
   in            inter            **super**
2. The king wanted to save money, but the queen wanted to host an eleg_____ affair.
   in            ous              **ant**
3. The queen convinced the king to spend the money because the event would _____ fit the poor.
   **bene**      trans            scrib
4. The queen thought the event would be adventur_____.
   ic            **ous**          it
5. The king thought the event would be too much to man_____.
   eous          ize              **age**
6. The queen thought a masquerade ball would be myster_____.
   eous          **ious**         ous
7. She wanted the guards dressed in _____form.
   **uni**       super            micro
8. The king tried not to be _____patient with her ideas.
   in            il               **im**

Step 2 Solutions
1. **interloper**
   cyclist       traveler         **intruder**
2. **imperceptible**
   uncatchable   **impossible to perceive**   not perfect
3. **transcutaneous**
   **across skin**   between cuts    above skin
4. **superscript**
   small words   **writing that's above**   one letter
5. **bounteous**
   see clearly   to make more     **full of bounty**
6. **ubiquity**
   make present  **quality of being everywhere**   causing to quit
7. **portage**
   shipping fee  **carrying of boat or cargo**   observing a port
8. **synchronize**
   timeless      not at same time   **causing at same time**

Step 3 Solutions
1. The king wondered if the park had an electrical out<u>age</u>.
2. He expected that the park would apolo<u>gize</u> for closing early.
3. He found the whole thing very myster<u>ious</u>.
4. The king promised he would deal with the park's dishones<u>ty</u>.
5. The king thought that his sending out the mission made Kirk nerv<u>ous</u>.
6. Ellen thought the Chrono <u>Trans</u>port would take them to a different time, but it was just a simple tram.
7. She was disappointed that she lost at <u>Inter</u> Balloon Darts, in which she tried to aim between the balloons.
8. Luke was also disappointed that he didn't get to ride high above the park on the <u>Super</u>sonic roller coaster.

**Mission 18: Spelling High-Frequency Words**

Dear guardians,

    If you struggle with spelling, you can be nervous about writing—especially to your friends. In this mission, you'll learn how to spell the most-used words that are also often misspelled. Then you can be a lot more confident in your writing. We are including a chart of these 35 words.

Sincerely,

*Kirk, Luke, and Ellen English*
Guardians of Grammar Galaxy

Mission 18: Spelling High-Frequency Words

| against | different | friend | probably | surprise |
|---|---|---|---|---|
| already | disease | government | receive | until |
| because | doesn't | instead | remember | weight |
| beginning | enough | million | rhythm | |
| believe | especially | necessary | separate | |
| business | exciting | notice | similar | |
| chief | experience | opposite | straight | |
| dictionary | finally | particular | studying | |

Mission 18: Spelling High-Frequency Words

## ★ Step 1: On Guard & Use Sayings to Remember Spellings
**On Guard.** *Read the sentences. Highlight the best answer.*

1. *Bene* means:
   collection           good           quality

2. One vocabulary mnemonic strategy is:
   song lyrics          onomatopoeia   oxymorons

3. When you are <u>leaving</u> a country, you are:
   immigrating          emigrating

4. The British English word for *sweater* is:
   hoarding             lorry          jumper

5. The British English spelling is:
   likable              likeable       likible

**Say each of these words in a sentence.** *Examples are given.*

| **astutely** – wisely | My grandmother **astutely** reminds us of the value of cooking skills. |
|---|---|
| **shrill** – high-pitched | When my mother gets angry, her voice gets **shrill**. |
| **crossly** – irritably | I tend to answer **crossly** when I'm hungry. |

Mission 18: Spelling High-Frequency Words

**Repeat these sayings until they are familiar.** *Pay attention to the bold and underlined parts of the words as you learn the sayings. Then spell the words that are written phonetically on the next page without looking at the sayings. Your teacher may ask you to spell the words orally if you prefer.*

**beginning** – At the beg**inning** of the inning, my two eyes were on the three n's.

**believe** – I be**lie**ved the lie Eve told me.

**business** – I get no z's in my bu**si**n**ess** selling nets for less.

**different** – One way they are **diffe**r**ent** is they differ on the rent.

**finally** – Fin **fin**a**lly** became my ally.

**friend** – I am your fr**i**e**nd** to the end.

**government** – "Go Vern!" said the signs for his g**o****vern**ment election.

**million** – Her mother-in-law (MIL) won the lion's share of a **mil**l**ion** dollars.

Mission 18: Spelling High-Frequency Words

1. /ˈfīn(ə)lē/ _____

2. /ˈbiznəs/ _____

3. /ˈgəvər(n)mənt/ _____

4. /ˈdif(ə)rənt/ _____

5. /ˈmilyən/ _____

6. /frend/ _____

7. /bəˈginiNG/ _____

8. /bəˈlēv/ _____

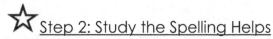 Step 2: Study the Spelling Helps

**Study the spelling helps.** *Pay attention to the spelling of each word. Then spell the words correctly next to the phonetic spellings on the following page. Don't peek! Your teacher may ask you to spell the words orally if you prefer.*

### because
Big Elephants Can Add Up Sums Easily
S says /z/ when a word ends in a vowel.

### chief / receive /weight
"i before e except after c or when sounded like /ay/ as in neighbor or weigh."
It is better to give than to receive.

### dictionary
Take action, Mary, and use a dictionary.

### disease
While sailing on the seas, he caught a di**seas**e but didn't die. (*Seas* is in the middle of the word *die*).
When two vowels are together, the first one usually says its name.
S says /z/ when a word ends in a vowel.

### doesn't
The doe isn't with her mate.
Doesn't is a contraction for *does not* with the apostrophe taking the place of the *o* and the *i* deleted.

### necessary
It is NECESSARY to have one (C)ollar and two (S)leeves.

### rhythm
Rhythm helps your two hips move.

### separate
There's a rat in separate.

Mission 18: Spelling High-Frequency Words

1. /ˈnesəˌserē/  _____

2. /CHēf/  _____

3. /dəˈzēz/  _____

4. /ˈsep(ə)rət/  _____

5. /ˈdikSHəˌnerē/  _____

6. /ˈdəz(ə)nt/  _____

7. /bēˈkəz/  _____

8. /ˈriTHəm/  _____

**Activity.** Give a family member a spelling test using the word list we sent you. How did they do?

## ⭐ Step 3: Study More Spelling Helps

**Study the spelling helps.** *Pay attention to the spelling of each word. Then spell the words correctly next to the phonetic spellings on the following page. Don't peek! Your teacher may ask you to spell the words orally if you prefer.*

**remember**
It's hard to remember who is a <u>member</u> of the group, but there are 3 people whose names start with <u>E</u>.

**straight**
<u>S</u>trong <u>A</u>rtificial <u>I</u>ntelligence <u>G</u>ets <u>H</u>umans <u>T</u>ogether

**studying**
He's only gotten one D because he's been stu<u>dy</u>ing.

**surprise**
<u>U</u> <u>R</u> w<u>ise</u> to keep it a surprise.
S says /z/ when a word ends in a vowel.

Mission 18: Spelling High-Frequency Words

1. /strāt/ _____

2. /sə(r)ˈprīz/ _____

3. /iˈnəf/ _____

4. /əˈgenst/ _____

5. /ˈstədē ing/ _____

6. /rəˈmembər/ _____

7. /ˈnōdəs/ _____

8. /ˌôlˈredē/ _____

**Vocabulary Victory!** Do you remember what these words mean? *Check Step 1 if you need a reminder.*

| astutely | "Kids don't always answer their communicators," Ellen said **astutely**. |
|---|---|
| shrill | "Did you invite anyone else?" Kirk asked in a **shrill** voice. |
| crossly | Without waiting for Luke to reply, he continued **crossly**. |

Mission 18: Spelling High-Frequency Words

☆ <u>Advanced Guardians Only</u>
**Write a message or email to friends using as many of the words from the high-frequency list as you can.** Be sure to spell them correctly. If you type it, save a copy to show your teacher. **Note:** <u>Be sure that the first letter of each sentence and the word I are capitalized</u>.

**Mission 18: Update**

Dear guardians,

    We are so impressed with your spelling skills! We hope you feel more confident when writing to friends and family.

    We didn't send you spelling helps for every word. Come up with your own mnemonic tricks for remembering to spell the rest. We are including the solutions for you to check.

Sincerely,

*Kirk, Luke, and Ellen English*
Guardians of Grammar Galaxy

P.S. You have completed all of the spelling and vocabulary missions! You're ready to take the challenge. You may want to review information from the guidebook for each mission before taking it.

Step 1 Solutions
**On Guard.**
1. *Bene* means:
   collection    good    quality
2. One vocabulary mnemonic strategy is:
   song lyrics    onomatopoeia    oxymorons
3. When you are leaving a country, you are:
   immigrating    emigrating
4. The British English word for *sweater* is:
   hoarding    lorry    jumper
5. The British English spelling is:
   likable    likeable    likible

**Repeat these sayings until they are familiar.**
1. /ˈfīn(ə)lē/    finally
2. /ˈbiznəs/    business
3. /ˈgəvər(n)mənt/    government
4. /ˈdif(ə)rənt/    different
5. /ˈmilyən/    million
6. /frend/    friend
7. /bəˈginiNG/    beginning
8. /bəˈlēv/    believe

Step 2 Solutions
1. /ˈnesəˌserē/    necessary
2. /CHēf/    chief
3. /dəˈzēz/    disease
4. /ˈsep(ə)rət/    separate
5. /ˈdikSHəˌnerē/    dictionary
6. /ˈdəz(ə)nt/    doesn't
7. /bēˈkəz/    because
8. /ˈriT͟Həm/    rhythm

Step 3 Solutions
1. /strāt/    straight
2. /sə(r)ˈprīz/    surprise
3. /iˈnəf/    enough
4. /əˈgenst/    against
5. /ˈstədē ing/    studying
6. /rəˈmembər/    remember
7. /ˈnōdəs/    notice
8. /ˌôlˈredē/    already

# Spelling & Vocabulary Challenge 1

*Carefully read all the possible answers* and then highlight the letter for the **one** best answer.

1. **The correct spelling for** /bəˈlēv/ **is:**
   a. beleev
   b. believ
   c. believe

2. **The root word** *scrib* **means:**
   a. cot
   b. write
   c. clean

3. **The word** *paramount* **means:**
   a. supreme
   b. superior
   c. both a and b

4. **The word meaning** *many* **is:**
   a. a lot
   b. alot
   c. allot

5. **The British word** *boot,* **as used in the story, means:**
   a. cowboy
   b. trunk
   c. kick

6. **The correct British spelling for someone who lives next door is:**
   a. naybour
   b. neighbor
   c. neighbour

Spelling & Vocabulary Challenge

7. **The word *screech* is an example of:**
   a. satire
   b. onomatopoeia
   c. an oxymoron

8. **The following is an oxymoron:**
   a. ice cold
   b. large fortune
   c. genuine imitation

9. **The science word root *omni* means:**
   a. over
   b. meat
   c. all

10. **The principal is your pal is an example of:**
    a. a mnemonic
    b. satire
    c. an oxymoron

Number Correct:_____/10

## ⭐ Advanced Guardian Vocabulary Challenge

For an extra challenge, highlight the word that best fits each blank.

1. The salesman who knocked on our door seemed _____ to us.
   sublime          shady          shaken

2. The _____ of serving fast food at a formal party was funny to us.
   vogue          requisite          incongruity

3. I had to _____ a laugh when my dad tripped.
   quash          shrill          soothe

4. Mother noted _____ that the game would be on sale again.
   shamefaced          profusely          astutely

5. Father said that the price was too _____.
   differentiated          steep          composed

6. My sister was warned not to be _____.
   impertinent          sentiment          sublime

7. The chipmunk in our yard _____ when it saw me.
   crossly          scurried          irked

8. Grandmother responded to our argument _____.
   numbly          charmed          judiciously

9. I hurt my brother's feelings, so I _____.
   recanted          composed          suppressed

Number Correct: _____ /9

Spelling & Vocabulary Challenge

★ Advanced Guardian Vocabulary Challenge
For an extra challenge, highlight the word that best fits each blank.

1. The salesman who knocked on our door seemed _____ to us.
   sublime        shady        sloven

2. The _____ of serving fast food at a formal party was funny to us.
   vogue         etiquette        incongruity

3. I had to _____ a laugh when my sister acted thieved.
   deport        smother        soothe

4. Mother noted _____ that the game would be a late match.
   mischievously       ruefully       astutely

5. Father said that the price was too _____.
   differential       inept       exorbitant

6. My sister was warned not to be _____ when speaking at funerals.
   impertinent       composed       audacious

7. The chipmunk in our yard _____ when it saw me.
   crouch       scurried       leapt

8. Grandmother responded to our argument _____.
   numbly       chained       indignantly

9. I hurt my brother's feelings so I _____.
   acceded       composed       apologized

   number of questions: __/9

Spelling & Vocabulary Challenge 1 Answers
1.c; 2.b; 3.c; 4.a; 5.b; 6.c; 7.b; 8.c; 9.c; 10.a

**If you got 9 or more correct, congratulations!** You've earned your Spelling & Vocabulary star. You may add it to your Grammar Guardian bookmark. You are ready for an adventure in grammar.

**If you did not get 9 or more correct, don't worry.** You have another chance. You may want to review the information in the guidebook for each story you've read so far. Then take the Spelling & Vocabulary Challenge 2. Remember to **choose the one best answer**.

Advanced Guardian Vocabulary Challenge Answers
1. shady
2. incongruity
3. quash
4. astutely
5. steep
6. impertinent
7. scurried
8. judiciously
9. recanted

# Spelling & Vocabulary Challenge 2

*Carefully read all the possible answers* and then highlight the letter for the **one** best answer.

1. **Using the complete i-before-e rule, which word is spelled <u>incorrectly</u>?**
    a. receive
    b. weigh
    c. both a and b are spelled correctly

2. **Ellen attempted to throw darts between balloons in the _____ Balloon Darts game:**
    a. Inter
    b. Among
    c. Throw

3. **Which word means *important in history*?**
    a. historic
    b. historical
    c. neither a nor b

4. **The British English word for pacifier is:**
    a. sucker
    b. dumb-dumb
    c. dummy

5. **The place to see a play in British English is the:**
    a. theater
    b. theatre
    c. theatur

6. **The following is onomatopoeia:**
    a. belch
    b. help
    c. yay

7. **Oxymorons are often used in:**
   a. science journals
   b. newspapers
   c. humor

8. **A chronometer measures:**
   a. time
   b. heat
   c. money

9. **The correct spelling is:**
   a. milion
   b. million
   c. millian

10. *uni-* **means:**
    a. college
    b. cyclist
    c. one

Number Correct:_____/10

## Spelling & Vocabulary Challenge 2 Answers
1.c; 2.a; 3.a; 4.c; 5.b; 6.a; 7.c; 8.a; 9.b; 10.c

**If you got 9 or more correct, congratulations!** You've earned your Spelling & Vocabulary star. You may add a star to your bookmark. You are now ready for an adventure in grammar.

**If you did not get 9 or more correct, don't worry.** Review the questions you missed with your teacher. You may want to get more practice using the resources at GrammarGalaxyBooks.com/BlueStar. Your teacher can ask you other questions like the ones you missed and if you get them correct, you'll have earned your Spelling & Vocabulary star and can move on to an adventure in grammar.

# Unit III: Adventures in Grammar

# OFFICIAL GUARDIAN MAIL

**Mission 19: Diagramming Sentences**

Dear guardian friends,

You may have seen our father's presentation for Diagramming Week. We know some people are fans of diagramming and some are not. But we agree with our father that diagramming can help some people understand grammar better.

Review the information on parts of speech and diagramming we are sending you. Then practice diagramming sentences. Whether you enjoy it or not, we hope you learn a lot.

Sincerely,

*Kirk, Luke, and Ellen English*
Guardians of Grammar Galaxy

---

**Subject** – The noun or pronoun doing or being.
<u>Luke</u> went home.
**Predicate** – What the subject is or does.
Luke <u>went</u> home.
**Direct Object** – Receives the action of a transitive verb.
Luke threw the <u>ball</u>.
**Adjective** – describe nouns
big, blue, good, four (includes the article adjectives *a*, *an*, *the*)
**Adverb** – explain verbs
slowly, later, outside

# Mission 19: Diagramming Sentences

1. **Simple subject and predicate**
**Josie chewed.**

Subject and predicate go on the horizontal line, separated by a vertical line.

2. **Direct object**
**Josie chewed bones.**

Direct object follows verb on horizontal line, separated by a top vertical line.

3. **Adjective**
**Little Josie chewed big bones.**

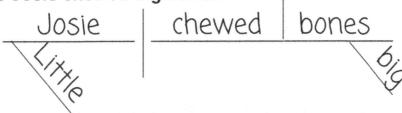

Adjectives are written on slanted lines under the nouns they modify.

4. **Adverb**
**Little Josie quickly chewed big bones.**

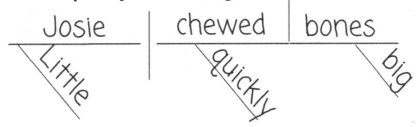

Adverbs are written on slanted lines under the verbs they modify.

Mission 19: Diagramming Sentences

⭐ Step 1: On Guard & Identify Incorrectly Diagrammed Sentences
**On Guard.** *Highlight the correct answer for the following sentence:*
<u>When Luke was on the Manchester interstate, he was suprised to see alot of hoardings.</u>

1. Which word has a prefix that means *between*?
   British                interstate                hoardings

2. Which of the words should be two words?
   Manchester             interstate                alot

3. Which word is misspelled?
   suprised               interstate                hoardings

4. Which word means *billboards*?
   Manchester             interstate                hoardings

5. If the word /ˈnābər/ had been on a Manchester hoarding, how would it have been spelled?
   neighbor               neighbour                 naber

**Say each of these words in a sentence.** *Examples are given.*

| **irked** – annoyed | I was **irked** that my friend didn't show up for my party. |
|---|---|
| **shady** – dishonest | Dad says my uncle is in a **shady** business. |
| **concession** – deal | Mom made the **concession** that I could buy a new game if I do extra chores. |

Mission 19: Diagramming Sentences

**Identify incorrectly diagrammed sentences.** *Look at the sentences and their diagrams below. Circle the diagram if it is NOT correct.*

1. **Luke laughed.**

2. **Luke laughed heartily.**

3. **Young Luke laughed heartily.**

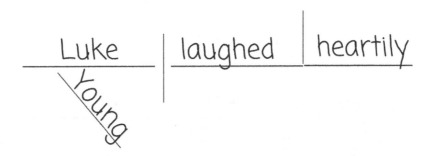

4. **Ellen cracked an egg.**

5. **Ellen quickly cracked an egg.**

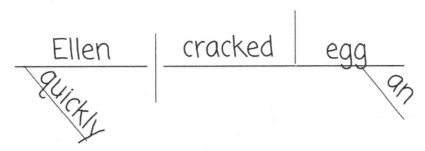

Mission 19: Diagramming Sentences

☆ Step 2: Write the Diagrammed Sentences
**Write the sentence above its diagram.** Be sure to add an end mark.

1. _____

   _____Kirk_____ | _____programmed_____

2. _____

   _____Cook_____ | _____made_____ | _____cookies_____

3. _____

   _____Luke_____ | _____read_____ | _____books_____
   \Young

4. _____

   _____Cook_____ | _____made_____ | _____cookies_____
                                              \sugar

5. _____

   _____Cook_____ | _____made_____ | _____lemonade_____
                       \also                    \pink

Mission 19: Diagramming Sentences

**Activity.** *Play a memory matching game, matching diagrams with sentences. Play with a friend or time yourself, using the cards below. You or your teacher should print the cards on cardstock and cut them out. A printable page may be found at GrammarGalaxyBooks.com/BlueStar. Put the cards face down and mix them up before playing.*

| | | |
|---|---|---|
| ——\|— | ——\|—\| | ——\|—\|<br>  \ |
| ——\|—\|<br>      \ | ——\|—\|<br>  \    \ | ——\|—\|<br>  \   \  \ |
| Cook decorated a cake. | Ellen made crafts. | Little Comet quickly ate steak bones. |
| Many guardians completed missions. | Guardians read. | Guardians carefully complete the mission. |

Mission 19: Diagramming Sentences

⭐ Step 3: Diagram the Sentences
**Diagram each sentence in the space below it.** *Refer to the graphic we sent you if you need help.*

1. Kirk likes robots.

2. Sweet Comet slept.

3. Kirk carefully added a piece.

4. Young guardians read many books.

5. Some kids play video games tirelessly.

**Vocabulary Victory!** Do you remember what these words mean? *Check Step 1 if you need a reminder.*

| irked | "I hated diagramming!" he declared, still **irked** by the protesting. |
|---|---|
| shady | He is probably paying these people to protest through one of his many **shady** organizations. |
| concession | These protesters are going to require some type of **concession**. |

Mission 19: Diagramming Sentences

**Write your own sentence for each diagram below.**

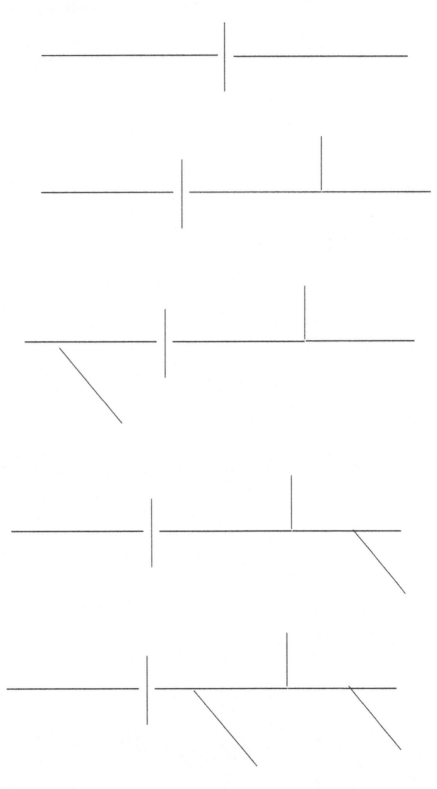

Mission 19: Diagramming Sentences

**Mission 19: Update**

Dear guardians,

    We hope you enjoyed Diagramming Week! We did. It's a new way of learning grammar. Father says to tell you that if diagramming helps you, there are more diagramming rules you can learn.

    Check the solutions to this mission to make sure you know how to diagram simple sentences.

Sincerely,

*Kirk, Luke, and Ellen English*
Guardians of Grammar Galaxy

## Mission 19: Diagramming Sentences

Step 1 Solutions

**On Guard.**

When Luke was on the Manchester interstate, he was suprised to see alot of hoardings.
1. Which word has a prefix that means *between*?
   British              interstate              hoardings
2. Which of the words should be two words?
   Manchester           interstate              alot
3. Which word is misspelled?
   suprised             interstate              hoardings
4. Which word means *billboards*?
   Manchester           interstate              hoardings
5. If the word /ˈnābər/ had been on a Manchester hoarding, how would it have been spelled?
   neighbor             neighbour               naber

**Identify incorrectly diagrammed sentences.**

1. Luke laughed.

   Luke | laughed

2. Luke laughed heartily.

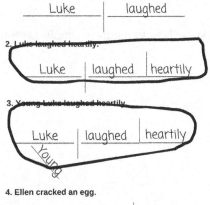

3. Young Luke laughed heartily.

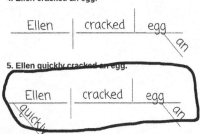

4. Ellen cracked an egg.

   Ellen | cracked | egg \ an

5. Ellen quickly cracked an egg.

   Ellen | cracked | egg \ an
   \ quickly

Step 2 Solutions

1. Kirk programmed.
2. Cook made cookies.
3. Young Luke read books.
4. Cook made sugar cookies.
5. Cook also made pink lemonade.

## Step 3 Solutions

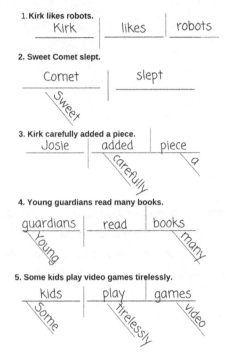

# OFFICIAL GUARDIAN MAIL

**Mission 20: Grammatical Mood**

Dear guardians,

Have you noticed that you phrase everything in the form of a question today? Did you notice that everyone was giving orders yesterday? Have we mentioned how much we appreciate you?

If our father can get the mood of the day ended on planet Sentence, will you be grateful? Are you ready to complete this mission on grammatical mood if we give you the information you need?

Sincerely,

*Kirk, Luke, and Ellen English*
Guardians of Grammar Galaxy

## Grammatical Mood

Grammatical mood is used to make the writer's or speaker's intention clear, primarily by the form and tone of the verb. There are five main types of grammatical mood.

**1) Interrogative mood** asks a question and uses helping verb forms of *be*, *do*, *is*, and *have*.
Are you going to camp?
When will you have enough money?

**2) Imperative mood** issues a command, often with the subject *you* understood but not specified.
(You) Grab me a tissue.
When you finish your math, start on your science.

**3) Indicative mood** makes statements of fact or belief.
I worry about kids who ride bikes without helmets.
There are about 100 million stars in the average galaxy.

**4) Conditional mood** is a statement that is dependent on conditions. It includes the helping verbs *would* and *should* and may use the if/then construction.
When we see the movie, we should get some popcorn.
If the concession stand is too busy, then I would skip the popcorn.

**5) Subjunctive mood** expresses a wish for something that may not be possible. The verb can indicate a desire, a suggestion, or a demand that may not be realized. The subjunctive uses the third-person (he, she, they) form of the verb without the *-s*, and it uses *be* rather than *is/are*. When describing a wish or a possibility, use *were* instead of *was*.
The teacher suggested that the student **seek** outside tutoring.
I desire that the students **be** heard.
If I **were** a millionaire, I'd buy a yacht.

## ★ Step 1: On Guard & Identify Grammatical Mood

**On Guard.** *Highlight TRUE or FALSE for each statement.*

1. The direct object is diagrammed on a slanted line.  TRUE  FALSE

2. *Separate* is a high-frequency, often-misspelled word.  TRUE  FALSE

3. *Port* means empty.  TRUE  FALSE

4. *Truculent* means quick to fight.  TRUE  FALSE

5. A complement is a thing that completes.  TRUE  FALSE

**Say each of these words in a sentence.** *Examples are given.*

| bustled – scurried | The staff **bustled** to get ready for the dinner rush. |
|---|---|
| amenable – agreeable | My parents seemed **amenable** to booking the trip. |
| ire – anger | I don't want to risk my brother's **ire** by taking his candy. |

**Identify grammatical mood.** *Read each sentence. Then highlight its grammatical mood. Use the verb and the information we sent you.*

1. After you finish the bathroom, wash the windows.
   interrogative     subjunctive     imperative

2. How do you think it went?
   interrogative     subjunctive     imperative

3. If you're finished asking questions, then I'll head to bed.
   interrogative     subjunctive     conditional

4. If I were king, I would put the Gremlin in the dungeon.
   interrogative     subjunctive     conditional

5. The Gremlin has caused most of the chaos in the galaxy.
   indicative     subjunctive     conditional

6. When I finish *Blue Star*, I would like to start *Nova*.
   indicative     subjunctive     conditional

7. The king suggested that Luke take his time reading.
   indicative     subjunctive     conditional

8. Grammar Galaxy needs more guardians like you.
   indicative     subjunctive     imperative

Mission 20: Grammatical Mood

⭐ Step 2: Choose the Correct Verb Form for the Subjunctive Mood

**Read each sentence that is written in the subjunctive mood below.** Highlight the verb form that belongs in the blank.

1. If I _____ you, I would get the chores done quickly.
   was            were

2. The queen suggested she _____ a cleaning cloth with her.
   take           takes

3. If I _____ a fairy godmother, I would use my magic wand to clean.
   were           was

4. The queen demanded that she _____ and finish.
   hurry          hurries

5. Luke wishes he _____ a better speller.
   was            were

6. It's been recommended that he _____ phonics.
   studies        study

7. His mother desires that he _____ more confident in spelling
   is             be

8. It's important that Luke _____ to study.
   agree          agrees

9. She asked that he _____ carefully during phonics time.
   listen         listens

10. He admitted that if he _____ a teacher, he would make spelling optional.
    was            were

**Activity.** *Play a game in Jeopardy® style where answers are given in interrogative mood.*

226

Mission 20: Grammatical Mood

☆ Step 3: Rewrite the Sentence in Another Mood
**Rewrite the sentence in the grammatical mood given in parentheses, using the line below.** *Note: You can use different words when you rewrite.*

1. Come with me, Comet! (interrogative)
___

2. What do you mean? (indicative)
___

3. Would you like to start your science when you finish your math? (imperative)
___

4. I would like some popcorn. (conditional)
___

5. I would buy a sports car. (subjunctive)
___

6. The teacher suggested he seek outside tutoring. (imperative)
___

7. When will you have enough money? (indicative)
___

8. I worry about kids who ride bikes without helmets. (conditional)
___

**Vocabulary Victory!** Do you remember what these words mean? *Check Step 1 if you need a reminder.*

| bustled | The queen **bustled** around, directing the family to do chores. |
| --- | --- |
| amenable | He hoped that being **amenable** would get chores over with sooner. |
| ire | He didn't want to raise his mother's **ire**. |

Mission 20: Grammatical Mood

☆ <u>Advanced Guardians Only</u>
*Write a paragraph all five grammatical moods. Write about chores, your feelings about spelling, or another topic of your choice. Be sure to indent your paragraph and start every sentence with a capital letter.*

# OFFICIAL GUARDIAN MAIL

**Mission 20: Update**

Dear guardian friends,

If you completed this mission, then we should be so proud of you! Don't worry. The conditional mood is not the mood of the day. Father was able to get the mood-of-the-day program canceled. We are glad, though we suspect our mother will be in an imperative mood the next time we have guests anyway.

We are proud of you for doing so well on your mission on grammatical mood. We are including the solutions to the mission for you to check.

Sincerely,

*Kirk, Luke, and Ellen English*
Guardians of Grammar Galaxy

Mission 20: Grammatical Mood

Step 1 Solutions
**On Guard.**
1. The direct object is diagrammed on a slanted line.     TRUE **FALSE**
2. *Separate* is a high-frequency, often-misspelled word.     **TRUE** FALSE
3. *Port* means empty.     TRUE **FALSE**
4. *Truculent* means quick to fight.     **TRUE** FALSE
5. A complement is a thing that completes.     **TRUE** FALSE

**Identify grammatical mood.**
1. After you finish the bathroom, wash the windows.
    interrogative     subjunctive     **imperative**
2. How do you think it went?
    **interrogative**     subjunctive     imperative
3. If you're finished asking questions, then I'll head to bed.
    interrogative     subjunctive     **conditional**
4. If I were king, I would put the Gremlin in the dungeon.
    interrogative     **subjunctive**     conditional
5. The Gremlin has caused most of the chaos in the galaxy.
    **indicative**     subjunctive     conditional
6. When I finish *Blue Star*, I would like to start *Nova*.
    indicative     subjunctive     **conditional**
7. The king suggested that Luke take his time reading.
    indicative     **subjunctive**     conditional
8. Grammar Galaxy needs more guardians like you.
    **indicative**     subjunctive     imperative

Step 2 Solutions
1. If I _____ you, I would get the chores done quickly.
    was     **were**
2. The queen suggested she _____ a cleaning cloth with her.
    **take**     takes
3. If I _____ a fairy godmother, I would use my magic wand to clean.
    **were**     was
4. The queen demanded that she _____ and finish.
    **hurry**     hurries
5. Luke wishes he _____ a better speller.
    was     **were**
6. It's been recommended that he _____ phonics.
    studies     **study**
7. His mother desires that he _____ more confident in spelling
    is     **be**
8. It's important that Luke _____ to study.
    **agree**     agrees
9. She asked that he _____ carefully during phonics time.
    **listen**     listens
10. He admitted that if he _____ a teacher, he would make spelling optional.
    was     **were**

Step 3 Solutions – answers may vary
1. **Come with me, Comet! (interrogative)** Do you want to come with me, Comet?
2. **What do you mean? (indicative)** I think I know what you mean.
3. **Would you like to start your science when you finish your math? (imperative)** Start your science when you finish your math.
4. **I would like some popcorn. (conditional)** If they have popcorn, I would like some.
5. **I would buy a sports car. (subjunctive)** If I were rich, I would buy a sports car.
6. **The teacher suggested he seek outside tutoring. (imperative)** Seek outside tutoring.
7. **When will you have enough money? (indicative)** I will have enough money next month.
8. **I worry about kids who ride bikes without helmets. (conditional)** When kids ride bikes without helmets, I worry.

**Mission 21: Infinitives**

Dear guardians,

If you've seen the new *Star Journey* movie, you might be repeating the phrase "to boldly go." But that might not be the only infinitive you've been using, to be clear.

Our father is trying to determine why infinitive use is on the rise. Until then, we need you to identify them and correct split infinitives. We are including information to help you.

Sincerely,

*Kirk, Luke, and Ellen English*
Guardians of Grammar Galaxy

## Infinitives

An infinitive is a noun, adjective, or adverb that is most commonly a combination of the word *to* and the simple form of the verb.

| | |
|---|---|
| to eat | I like to eat. (noun, direct object of *like*) |
| to read | I brought a book to read. (adjective, describes *book*) |
| to improve | I am studying to improve my vocabulary. (adverb, modifies studying) |

A **split infinitive** is an adverb placed between *to* and the simple verb. Split infinitives should be avoided in formal writing.

**to** carefully **put**
**to** boldly **go**

To correct a split infinitive, place the adverb before or after the infinitive, unless the new word order creates confusion.

Carefully, she started **to put** her dolls away.
We are determined **to go** boldly where no one has gone before.

Mission 21: Infinitives

## ⭐ Step 1: On Guard & Identify the Part of Speech of Infinitives

**On Guard.** *Answer the following questions or answer verbally for your teacher.*

1. What are the five grammatical moods?

2. Why should students be taught basic diagramming?

3. How many words are on the high-frequency word list that are also frequently misspelled?

4. What do the prefixes *il-*, *im-*, *in-*, and *ir-* mean?

5. Give two types of mnemonics for learning vocabulary.

**Say each of these words in a sentence.** *Examples are given.*

| **lauded** – praised | My brother's recital was **lauded** by the whole family. |
|---|---|
| **agenda** – schedule | A trip to the dentist is on our **agenda** for today. |
| **endeavor** – effort | Building forts was my favorite **endeavor** when I was younger. |

**Identify the part of speech of infinitives.** *Read the sentence. Highlight the part of speech of the underlined infinitive.* **Hint:** *Subjects and direct objects are nouns. Adverbs may answer the question why?*

1. I want <u>to go</u> where no one has gone before.
    direct object        adjective        adverb

2. The king wanted us <u>to create</u> a mission.
    direct object        adjective        adverb

3. <u>To defeat</u> the Gremlin is our mission.
    subject            adjective        adverb

4. We are writing <u>to teach</u> you about infinitives.
    subject            adjective        adverb

5. This is a mission <u>to check</u> your knowledge of parts of speech.
    direct object        adjective        adverb

6. Reading is the way <u>to protect</u> the galaxy.
    direct object        adjective        adverb

7. We also read <u>to improve</u> our spelling.
    direct object        adjective        adverb

8. <u>To guard</u> the galaxy is our job.
    subject            adjective        adverb

⭐ Step 2: Identify Split Infinitives
**Read each sentence and highlight the split infinitive.**

1. To boldly go to the next level in my video game is my mission today.

2. To heartily workout is a worthy endeavor.

3. To suddenly be summoned is alarming.

4. Are you sure this is something you want to really focus on?

5. Something is causing us to excessively use infinitives.

6. Father is ready to carefully assess the problem.

7. We hope he will be able to easily determine its source.

8. Until he does, we need to diligently work on our mission.

**Activity.** *Watch the Star Trek original series intro (see GrammarGalaxyBooks.com/BlueStar). How many infinitives are a part of the Enterprise's mission? How many of the infinitives are split?*

Mission 21: Infinitives

⭐ Step 3: Rewrite Sentences That Have Split Infinitives
**Rewrite each sentence in the space below it, keeping the infinitive but placing the adverb so it does not create a split.**

1. To boldly go to the next level in my video game is my mission today.

2. To heartily work out is a worthy endeavor.

3. To suddenly be summoned is alarming.

4. Are you sure this is something you want to really focus on?

5. Something is causing us to excessively use infinitives.

6. Father is ready to carefully assess the problem.

7. We hope he will be able to easily determine its source.

8. Until he does, we need to diligently work on our mission.

**Vocabulary Victory!** Do you remember what these words mean? *Check Step 1 if you need a reminder.*

| lauded | When they **lauded** the film, she told them she couldn't wait to see it. |
|---|---|
| agenda | What do you have on your **agenda** for today? |
| endeavor | To work out is a worthy **endeavor**. |

Mission 21: Infinitives

☆ **Advanced Guardians Only**
**Write a description of a movie you saw recently, using an infinitive as a noun, an adjective, and an adverb.**

Mission 21: Infinitives

**Mission 21: Update**

Dear guardians,

    Our father was able to determine that the new *Star Journey* movie was responsible for infinitive overuse on planet Sentence. "To boldly go" became such a popular phrase that the other sentences wanted to be in the spotlight, too. He says that there is nothing we need to do for now. It's a fad that will likely fade. But he is happy that we all know about infinitives and not to split them if we can help it.

    Please check the solutions we are sending to make sure you have them mastered.

Sincerely,

*Kirk, Luke, and Ellen English*
Guardians of Grammar Galaxy

Mission 21: Infinitives

Step 1 Solutions
**On Guard.**
1. **What are the five grammatical moods?** Interrogative, imperative, indicative, conditional, subjunctive
2. **Why should students be taught basic diagramming?** It may help visual learners understand grammar.
3. **How many words are on the high-frequency word list that are also frequently misspelled?** 35
4. **What do the prefixes *il-*, *im-*, *in-*, and *ir-* mean?** not
5. **Give two types of mnemonics for learning vocabulary.** Sayings, word pictures, songs, premade

**Identify the part of speech of infinitives.**
1. I want to go where no one has gone before.
   **direct object**     adjective     adverb
2. The king wanted us to create a mission.
   direct object     adjective     **adverb**
3. To defeat the Gremlin is our mission.
   **subject**     adjective     adverb
4. We are writing to teach you about infinitives.
   subject     adjective     **adverb**
5. This is a mission to check your knowledge of parts of speech.
   direct object     **adjective**     adverb
6. Reading is the way to protect the galaxy.
   direct object     **adjective**     adverb
7. We also read to improve our spelling.
   direct object     adjective     **adverb**
8. To guard the galaxy is our job.
   **subject**     adjective     adverb

Step 2 Solutions
1. **To boldly go** to the next level in my video game is my mission today.
2. **To heartily workout** is a worthy endeavor.
3. **To suddenly be summoned** is alarming.
4. Are you sure this is something you want **to really focus** on?
5. Something is causing us **to excessively use** infinitives.
6. Father is ready **to carefully assess** the problem.
7. We hope he will be able **to easily determine** its source.
8. Until he does, we need **to diligently work** on our mission.

Step 3 Solutions – answers will vary
1. **To boldly go to the next level in my video game is my mission today.**
To go boldly to the next level in my video game is my mission today.
2. **To heartily work out is a worthy endeavor.**
To work out heartily is a worthy endeavor.
3. **To suddenly be summoned is alarming.**
To be summoned suddenly is alarming.
4. **Are you sure this is something you want to really focus on?**
Are you sure this is something you really want to focus on?
5. **Something is causing us to excessively use infinitives.**
Something is causing us to use infinitives excessively.
6. **Father is ready to carefully assess the problem.**
Father is ready to assess the problem carefully.
7. **We hope he will be able to easily determine its source.**
We hope he will easily be able to determine its source.
8. **Until he does, we need to diligently work on our mission.**
Until he does, we need to work diligently on our mission.

**Mission 22: Progressive Tense**

Dear guardians,

This mission is a little unusual for us. We are completing it as a surprise for our father. He has been very upset about the progressives. We will include information to help you identify the progressive tense. Our plan is to send these progressive verbs to planet Recycling where they won't cause problems for our father any longer.

Are you in? We'll be waiting for your completed mission so we can take action. Then we can give the good news to our father.

Gratefully,

*Kirk, Luke, and Ellen English*
Guardians of Grammar Galaxy

## Progressive Tense

The progressive tense is used to show that a verb's action is in progress and ongoing. The progressive tense is constructed of the helping verb *be* plus the present participle form of the verb (-ing).

There are six progressive tenses: present, past, future, present perfect, past perfect, and future perfect. The table below compares the progressive tenses to the standard tenses.

| Tense | Progressive | Standard |
| --- | --- | --- |
| Present | She **is reading** the book. | She **reads** the book. |
| Past | She **was reading** the book. | She **read** the book. |
| Future | She **will be reading** the book. | She **will read** the book. |
| Present Perfect | She **has been reading** the book. | She **has read** the book. |
| Past Perfect | She **had been reading** the book. | She **had read** the book. |
| Future Perfect | She **will have been reading** the book. | She **will have read** the book. |

Mission 22: Progressive Tense

## ★ Step 1: On Guard & Identify Progressive Tense
**On Guard.** *Highlight TRUE or FALSE for each statement.*

1. Most infinitives begin with the word *to*.     TRUE   FALSE

2. An if/then statement is written in the indicative mood.     TRUE   FALSE

3. An adjective is diagrammed under the verb of the sentence.     TRUE   FALSE

4. The word <u>goverment</u> is spelled correctly.     TRUE   FALSE

5. The suffixes *-eous, -ious, -ous* mean full of or characterized by.     TRUE   FALSE

**Say each of these words in a sentence.** *Examples are given.*

| **accessible** – user-friendly | Our new TV controls aren't very **accessible**. |
|---|---|
| **impede** – hinder | The road construction worked to **impede** our progress. |
| **usurp** – take | Our coach has said he will not let a parent **usurp** his authority. |

Mission 22: Progressive Tense

**Identify progressive tense.** *Read each sentence. Highlight the sentence if it is written in progressive tense.*

1. The king has been complaining about progressives in Parliament.

2. The queen has tried to calm him without success.

3. The children have not seen him this upset.

4. Kirk, Luke, and Ellen have been researching the progressive tense.

5. What they learned has convinced them to take action.

6. They will be waiting on planet Sentence for the guardians' missions.

7. They will have been waiting a short time if the guardians work quickly.

8. The king had not been expecting the children to send a mission.

⭐ Step 2: Identify the Tense of Each Sentence
**Read each sentence.** *Then highlight which tense it is written in.* **Hint:** *The progressive tense uses a participle ending in -ing.*

1. **The king reads the paper every day.**
   present         past perfect            present progressive

2. **The queen was reading on her tablet when the king complained.**
   present         past progressive        past perfect

3. **The queen had been hoping the king wouldn't read the paper.**
   past            past perfect            past perfect progressive

4. **The king enjoyed the quiz show.**
   past            past progressive        present

5. **Comet has been enjoying the petting.**
   present         past perfect            present perfect progressive

6. **The children wondered what to do.**
   present         past                    past perfect progressive

7. **The king will be waking up soon.**
   present         future progressive      future perfect

8. **The king will have been waiting for the children to return home.**
   future          future perfect          future perfect progressive


**Activity.** *Say each of the sentences in the chart we sent you, substituting **He** as the subject, **play** as the verb, and **game** as the direct object. For the present progressive tense, you would say, "He is playing the game."*

Mission 22: Progressive Tense

## ⭐ Step 3: Rewrite Sentences in Standard Tense

**Read each sentence that is written in progressive tense.** *Determine which progressive tense it is written in. Then rewrite the sentence in standard tense on the line below.* **Hint:** *Use the chart we sent you to help you.*

1. The king is getting upset about the news.
   _____

2. The queen was trying to calm him.
   _____

3. The children had been hoping that the show would cheer him.
   _____
   _____

4. Comet will be hoping he is in a better mood.
   _____

5. Kirk, Luke, and Ellen are wanting to surprise him.
   _____

6. They will be working quickly.
   _____

7. The king had been thinking he was overreacting.
   _____

8. The king will have been waiting for the children.
   _____

**Vocabulary Victory!** Do you remember what these words mean? *Check Step 1 if you need a reminder.*

| accessible | English needs to be **accessible**. |
|---|---|
| impede | "Dear…" the queen said to try to **impede** the coming explosion. |
| usurp | They are trying to **usurp** my authority. |

☆ Advanced Guardians Only

**Write about something that upsets you, using all six progressive tenses.** *Put an X in front of each tense as you use it. Then we will send what you wrote to planet Recycling.*

|   |                              |
|---|------------------------------|
|   | Present Progressive          |
|   | Past Progressive             |
|   | Future Progressive           |
|   | Present Perfect Progressive  |
|   | Past Perfect Progressive     |
|   | Future Perfect Progressive   |

**Mission 22: Update**

Dear guardians,

    We are embarrassed to admit that we did something very wrong. We didn't talk to our father before we sent out this mission. While you are not at fault, Father is upset that we sent hundreds of progressive verbs to planet Recyling. We are on our way to get them back to planet Sentence where they belong.

    Father explained that he was upset about progressive grammar, not progressive verb tenses. Progressive grammar means changing rules to keep up with changes in a society. After time spent thinking, he now says he agrees that some grammar rule changes should be made. While he is not happy that we didn't talk to him, he understands that we were trying to help.

    The good news is we all learned something from this. Even though we have to return the verbs, we would like you to review your mission solutions.

Sincerely,

*Kirk, Luke, and Ellen English*
Guardians of Grammar Galaxy

P.S. Father said to tell you not to worry if you didn't get some of your mission questions correct. Progressive tense takes lots of practice.

Mission 22: Progressive Tense

Step 1 Solutions

**On Guard.**
1. Most infinitives begin with the word *to*. — **TRUE** FALSE
2. An if/then statement is written in the indicative mood. — **TRUE** FALSE
3. An adjective is diagrammed under the verb of the sentence. — TRUE **FALSE**
4. The word <u>goverment</u> is spelled correctly. — TRUE **FALSE**
5. The suffixes *-eous, -ious, -ous* mean full of or characterized by. — **TRUE** FALSE

**Identify progressive tense.**
1. <mark>The king has been complaining about progressives in Parliament.</mark>
2. The queen has tried to calm him without success.
3. The children have not seen him this upset.
4. <mark>Kirk, Luke, and Ellen have been researching the progressive tense.</mark>
5. What they learned has convinced them to take action.
6. <mark>They will be waiting on planet Sentence for the guardians' missions.</mark>
7. <mark>They will have been waiting a short time if the guardians work quickly.</mark>
8. <mark>The king had not been expecting the children to send a mission.</mark>

Step 2 Solutions

1. The king reads the paper every day.
   **present**     past perfect     present progressive
2. The queen was reading on her tablet when the king complained.
   present     **past progressive**     past perfect
3. The queen had been hoping the king wouldn't read the paper.
   past     past perfect     **past perfect progressive**
4. The king enjoyed the quiz show.
   **past**     past progressive     present
5. Comet has been enjoying the petting.
   present     past perfect     **present perfect progressive**
6. The children wondered what to do.
   present     **past**     past perfect progressive
7. The king will be waking up soon.
   present     **future progressive**     future perfect
8. The king will have been waiting for the children to return home.
   future     future perfect     **future perfect progressive**

Step 3 Solutions

1. The king is getting upset about the news.
   <u>The king gets upset about the news.</u>
2. The queen was trying to calm him.
   <u>The queen tried to calm him.</u>
3. The children had been hoping that the show would cheer him.
   <u>The children had hoped that the show would cheer him.</u>
4. Comet will be hoping he is in a better mood.
   <u>Comet will hope he is in a better mood.</u>
5. Kirk, Luke, and Ellen are wanting to surprise him.
   <u>Kirk, Luke, and Ellen want to surprise him.</u>
6. They will be working quickly.
   <u>They will work quickly.</u>
7. The king had been thinking he was overreacting.
   <u>The king had thought he was overreacting.</u>
8. The king will have been waiting for the children.
   <u>The king will have waited for the children.</u>

**Mission 23: Adverbial Clauses & Phrases**

Dear guardians,

     Wherever you are. As long as it takes. While adverbial causes and phrases are being overused. On planet Sentence. Because of *TheyDunnit*.

     Please complete this mission. Until Father gets the show to stop airing. We've included information you'll need.

Sincerely,

*Kirk, Luke, and Ellen English*
Guardians of Grammar Galaxy

### Adverbial Clauses & Phrases

**Adverbial phrases** are groups of words that function as adverbs (communicating where, when, how, or why) that don't include both a subject and predicate. They may be prepositional phrases, infinitives, or an adverb pairing.

I can read **in the car**. (prepositional phrase communicating where)
I like reading **to pass the time**. (adverb communicating why)
I like reading mysteries **very quickly**. (adverb pairing communicating how)

**Adverbial clauses** are dependent clauses that include both a subject and predicate, or these are understood from the sentence.

Some common conjunctions used in adverbial clauses are listed in the chart below.

| Communicates | Conjunctions | Example |
| --- | --- | --- |
| Where | anywhere, everywhere, where, wherever | I like to read **wherever I can find a comfy spot**. |
| When | after, as long as, before, since, when, while, until | I like to read **before I go to bed**. |
| How | although, as, if, like, though, unless, while | I read **as quietly as I can if I am up late**. |
| Why | because, given, in order to, since, so that | I stay up late reading **because I want to finish the book**. |

Mission 23: Adverbial Clauses & Phrases

## ⭐ Step 1: On Guard & Identify Clauses & Phrases
**On Guard.** *Highlight the correct answer for each statement.*

1. Which verb is in progressive tense?
   ate                              will be eating

2. Which of these is an infinitive?
   to eat                           will have been eating

3. Which sentence is in the subjunctive mood?
   I wish that children be given books as gifts.
   Hand me my book.

4. Which sentence would be diagrammed without a slanted line?
   Children enjoy ball games.
   Kids climb trees.

5. Which word is spelled <u>incorrectly</u>?
   believe                          allready

**Say each of these words in a sentence.** *Examples are given.*

| **depicted** – showed | The preview **depicted** the movie as an action film. |
|---|---|
| **palatial** – grand | The open staircase makes the theater appear **palatial**. |
| **intoned** – spoke | We grew more restless the longer the announcer **intoned**. |

Mission 23: Adverbial Clauses & Phrases

**Identify clauses and phrases.** *Highlight whether each underlined group of words is a clause or phrase.* **Hint:** *Clauses have both a subject (noun) and a predicate (verb).*

1. The kids had to help clean up <u>because they had disobeyed their parents</u>.
    clause                  phrase

2. <u>As soon as dinner was over</u>, they got to work.
    clause                  phrase

3. But they loved cleaning <u>to help Cook</u>.
    clause                  phrase

4. Cook loved having them <u>in the kitchen</u>.
    clause                  phrase

5. The queen was concerned, <u>though the show wasn't scary</u>.
    clause                  phrase

6. The children finished their work <u>very quickly</u>.
    clause                  phrase

7. They wanted to be ready <u>to watch the show</u>.
    clause                  phrase

8. They knew they couldn't watch <u>unless their parents approved</u>.
    clause                  phrase

## ⭐ Step 2: Find the Adverbial Clause or Phrase
**Read each sentence.** *Then highlight the adverbial clause or phrase in each.*

1. *TheyDunnit* was filmed where the crime took place.

2. The show's host was shown in a cornfield.

3. To increase the mystery, the background was blurred.

4. After the commercial, the scene switched to main street.

5. The host said the location was "hot" to give a clue.

6. While he spoke, people entered a brick building.

7. Luke thought it was a bank, though he wasn't sure.

8. So that viewers would keep tuning in, very few clues were given.

**Activity.** *Play a game of Cold-Warm-Hot with your teacher, a sibling, or a friend, using a reward you've hidden. Use an adverbial phrase or clause each time you say cold, warm, or hot. For example, "When you take two steps forward, you'll be hot."*

⭐ Step 3: Write Complete Sentences with Adverbial Clauses

**Adverbial clauses are not complete sentences.** *Add to them so they make sense. Review the story for ideas.*

1. After the commercial plays, _____
_____.

2. If they don't give us more clues, _____
_____.

3. _____ where he was.

4. _____ as if he would never be caught.

5. _____
because no one is making sense.

6. If I could have a report from planet Sentence, _____
_____.

7. As the show's popularity increased, _____
_____.

8. Unless we do something, _____
_____.

**Vocabulary Victory!** Do you remember what these words mean? *Check Step 1 if you need a reminder.*

| depicted | The story **depicted** a man who had successfully stolen five million dollars. |
| --- | --- |
| palatial | The man gave the camera crew a tour of the **palatial** home he'd purchased with the money. |
| intoned | "I'm here in the place where our criminal stole five million dollars," he **intoned** dramatically. |

Mission 23: Adverbial Clauses & Phrases

☆ Advanced Guardians Only

**We don't want planet Sentence to be upset when *TheyDunnit* stops airing there.** Write where, when, and how you think the thief stole the money using adverbial clauses and phrases. We think that will keep them happy.

Mission 23: Adverbial Clauses & Phrases

**Mission 23: Update**

Dear guardians,

    Thank you! We are back to speaking in complete sentences because of your completed mission. The words on planet Sentence loved getting your theories on where, when, and how the thief of *TheyDunnit* stole the money. It helped that you used adverbial clauses and phrases, too! There have been no complaints that the show isn't airing on the planet. That's a relief. These clauses and phrases are important to solving mysteries, so we will keep checking your knowledge of them in future missions.

Sincerely,

*Kirk, Luke, and Ellen English*
Guardians of Grammar Galaxy

P.S. We are including the solutions to this mission.

Mission 23: Adverbial Clauses & Phrases

Step 1 Solutions
**On Guard.**
1. Which verb is in progressive tense?
    ate    will be eating
2. Which of these is an infinitive?
    to eat    will have been eating
3. Which sentence is in the subjunctive mood?
    I wish that children be given books as gifts.
    Hand me my book.
4. Which sentence would be diagrammed without a slanted line?
    Children enjoy ball games.
    Kids climb trees.
5. Which word is spelled incorrectly?
    believe    allready

**Identify clauses and phrases.**
1. The kids had to help clean up because they had disobeyed their parents.
    clause    phrase
2. As soon as dinner was over, they got to work.
    clause    phrase
3. But they loved cleaning to help Cook.
    clause    phrase
4. Cook loved having them in the kitchen.
    clause    phrase
5. The queen was concerned, though the show wasn't scary.
    clause    phrase
6. The children finished their work very quickly.
    clause    phrase
7. They wanted to be ready to watch the show.
    clause    phrase
8. They knew they couldn't watch unless their parents approved.
    clause    phrase

Step 2 Solutions
1. *TheyDunnit* was filmed where the crime took place.
2. The show's host was shown in a cornfield.
3. To increase the mystery, the background was blurred.
4. After the commercial, the scene switched to main street.
5. The host said the location was "hot" to give a clue.
6. While he spoke, people entered a brick building.
7. Luke thought it was a bank, though he wasn't sure.
8. So that viewers would keep tuning in, very few clues were given.

Step 3 Solutions – answers will vary
1. After the commercial plays, they'll give us more clues.
2. If they don't give us more clues, we won't know where he stole the money.
3. The blurred background didn't help us identify where he was.
4. The thief bragged as if he would never be caught.
5. Something is wrong because no one is making sense.
6. If I could have a report from planet Sentence, I could identify the problem.
7. As the show's popularity increased, people began using more adverbial phrases and clauses.
8. Unless we do something, we won't be able to communicate.

**Mission 24: Relative Pronouns**

Dear guardians,

    We are interrupting our mother's family reunion to send out an urgent mission. The Gremlin sent an invitation to another family reunion on planet Sentence. Relative pronouns are attending, making them unavailable to us here. We need your help to identify them. Grammar Patrol will get them back to work. Thanks in advance!

Sincerely,

*Kirk, Luke, and Ellen English*
Guardians of Grammar Galaxy

P.S. We are sending you information on relative pronouns that you will need.

## Relative Pronouns

A relative pronoun begins an adjective clause. An adjective clause is a dependent or subordinate clause, providing more information about a noun (also called the antecedent). The most common relative pronouns are *that*, *which*, *who*, *whose*, and *whom*. The pronouns *that* and *which* are <u>not</u> used to refer to people.

**This is the book that got Joe interested in reading.**
*The clause beginning with <u>that</u> describes <u>book</u>.*
**She is the librarian who told me about this series.**
*The clause beginning with <u>who</u> describes <u>librarian</u>.*

**If the adjective clause is not essential in identification or to the sentence's meaning, it is set apart with commas.** *If we know specifically who or what without the clause, it is nonessential. <u>That</u> is always used to introduce an essential clause.*

**Natalie, who wears her hair in pigtails, likes reading picture books.** (not essential)
**Books that include new vocabulary words improving reading skills.** (essential)

Mission 24: Relative Pronouns

## ★ Step 1: On Guard & Identify Adjective Clauses
**On Guard.** *Answer the questions or answer verbally for your teacher.*

1. What is the difference between an adverbial clause and phrase?

2. What is the progressive tense used to show?

3. What three parts of speech can an infinitive serve as?

4. What are three grammatical moods?

5. What must you know before you diagram a sentence?

**Say each of these words in a sentence.** *Examples are given.*

| vexation – annoyance | Finding my dirty socks on the floor is a **vexation** to my mother. |
|---|---|
| curtly – tersely | The busy cashier answered our question **curtly**. |
| disconcerted – perturbed | Dad's failure to answer his phone has Mom **disconcerted**. |

**Identify Adjective Clauses.** *Read each sentence. Highlight the adjective clause that begins with a relative pronoun.* **Note:** <u>An adjective clause has both a subject and a predicate.</u>

1. This is the house that the queen's grandfather built.

2. The queen's cousin, who is closest to her in age, greeted her first.

3. The man whom she married was a friend of the king.

4. Kathy, whose recreational vehicle is parked nearby, brought cookies for everyone.

5. Mother was looking for any cousin whose information wasn't in the scrapbook.

6. Second cousins are children who are born to mother's cousins.

7. We met our mother's cousin, who asked us to call her Jo.

8. The reunion ends this Sunday, which is also her father's birthday.

Mission 24: Relative Pronouns

⭐ Step 2: Add Commas to Nonessential Adjective Clauses

**Read each sentence.** *Decide whether the underlined adjective clause is essential or nonessential. If it is nonessential (not needed for specific identification or for the sentence to make sense), add commas to set off the clause.*

1. Many cousins brought pictures <u>that could be added to a family scrapbook</u>.

2. Betty <u>whose hobby is family history</u> brought all of her research.

3. Anyone <u>who wanted the extra pictures she brought</u> could take them.

4. Before we left, Luke had fun playing with a boy <u>who brought spaceball equipment</u>.

5. Blackberry pie <u>which is his favorite</u> drew the king to the dessert table.

6. Luke felt bad about leaving Comet <u>whose tail wagging added to his guilt</u>.

7. "This is my dog <u>that competes in frisbee competitions</u>," a cousin said.

8. "We are looking for anyone <u>whose information was left out of the scrapbook</u>," the queen said.

**Activity.** *Ask parents or grandparents to show you old family photos and tell you about their cousins. Note how many relative pronouns they use as they do.*

Mission 24: Relative Pronouns

⭐ Step 3: Complete Sentences with an Adjective Clause
**Imagine that you are sharing pictures at a family reunion.** *Complete the adjective clauses that you would use in the quotes below.*

1. "This is my house that_____."

2. "My mother, who _____, is over there."

3. "You should meet my _____, who _____
_____."

4. "We traveled by _____, which_____
_____."

5. "Apple pie, which_____, is what we brought to the picnic."

6. "I see my cousin _____, who_____
_____, quite often."

7. "Anyone who_____
with us can."

8. "This is the picture that_____."


**Vocabulary Victory!** Do you remember what these words mean? *Check Step 1 if you need a reminder.*

| vexation | "The whole weekend?" the king asked, trying to hide his **vexation**. |
|---|---|
| curtly | "Yes, the whole weekend," she answered **curtly**. |
| disconcerted | She was **disconcerted** by her family's slowness in getting ready. |

Mission 24: Relative Pronouns

☆ Advanced Guardians Only

**Share information about your family that could be included in a cousin scrapbook.** *Type it, write by hand on the lines below, or film a video. Be sure to use relative pronouns.*

Mission 24: Relative Pronouns

**Mission 24: Update**

Dear guardian friends,

We are so grateful to you because our mother was able to enjoy her cousins' reunion. With your help, Grammar Patrol was able to break up the picnic on planet Sentence. Relative pronouns that begin adjective clauses are usable once again.

We really enjoyed meeting our mother's cousins and we loved learning about your families, too. We are including the solutions to your mission for your review. Be looking for relative pronouns that may have stayed at the picnic!

Sincerely,

*Kirk, Luke, and English*
Guardians of Grammar Galaxy

Mission 24: Relative Pronouns

Step 1 Solutions

**On Guard.**

1. **What is the difference between an adverbial clause and phrase?** A clause has a subject and a predicate and a phrase does not.

2. **What is the progressive tense used to show?** Verb's action is in progress and ongoing.

3. **What three parts of speech can an infinitive serve as?** Noun, adjective, adverb

4. **What are three grammatical moods?** Interrogative, indicative, conditional, subjunctive, imperative

5. **What must you know before you diagram a sentence?** Parts of speech

**Identify adjective clauses.**

1. This is the house that the queen's grandfather built.
2. The queen's cousin, who is closest to her in age, greeted her first.
3. The man whom she married was a friend of the king.
4. Kathy, whose recreational vehicle is parked nearby, brought cookies for everyone.
5. Mother was looking for any cousin whose information wasn't in the scrapbook.
6. Second cousins are children who are born to mother's cousins.
7. We met our mother's cousin, who asked us to call her Jo.
8. The reunion ends this Sunday, which is also her father's birthday.

Step 2 Solutions

1. Many cousins brought pictures that could be added to a family scrapbook.
2. Betty, whose hobby is family history, brought all of her research.
3. Anyone who wanted the extra pictures she brought could take them.
4. Before we left, Luke had fun playing with a boy who brought spaceball equipment.
5. Blackberry pie, which is his favorite, drew the king to the dessert table.
6. Luke felt bad about leaving Comet, whose tail wagging added to his guilt.
7. "This is my dog that competes in frisbee competitions," a cousin said.
8. "We are looking for anyone whose information was left out of the scrapbook," the queen said.

**Mission 25: Misplaced Modifiers**

Dear guardians,

    We don't know if your parents have read the *Galaxy Life* article about our father or not. But we wanted you to know that there is a problem with it: misplaced modifiers. They can be confusing.

    Father experienced sentence coordinators that have been replaced. That's not right. Let's just say that there is a problem on planet Sentence with misplaced modifiers, and we need your help. We are sending you misplaced modifiers on a mission. We hope you know what we mean.

Sincerely,

*Kirk, Luke, and Ellen English*
Guardians of Grammar Galaxy

## Misplaced Modifiers

Words, phrases, or clauses that are separated from the word they explain can result in an uncertain meaning. These are called misplaced modifiers. Correcting them involves moving the modifier, so it is next to the word it modifies.

**A misplaced modifier may be an adjective.**

She found an expensive woman's shirt at the thrift store. – *misplaced; the woman isn't expensive.*

She found a woman's expensive shirt at the thrift store. – *correct*

**Misplaced modifiers can be adverbs.**

She opened the gift they gave her slowly. – *misplaced; they didn't give her the gift slowly.*

She slowly opened the gift they gave her. – *correct*

**Misplaced modifiers can be phrases or clauses.**

The boy put the hot dog in the trash he had eaten. – *incorrect; the boy hadn't eaten the trash.*

The boy put the hot dog he had eaten in the trash. – *correct*

The child held a snake in his room made of clay. – *incorrect, the room isn't made of clay.*

In his room, the child held a snake made of clay. – *correct*

**Dangling modifiers (also called dangling participles) are -ing verbs that often come at the beginning of sentences.** They cannot be corrected simply by moving them in the sentence. To correct them, either add the word being modified or change the dangling modifier to a subordinate clause.

Looking around the library, new books were everywhere. – *incorrect; the new books weren't looking around.*

Looking around the library, I saw new books everywhere. – *correct, added the word being modified (I).*

Rotting in the basement, my brother brought up a case of apples. – *incorrect; your brother wasn't rotting in the basement.*

My brother brought up a case of apples that he found rotting in the basement. – *correct; added a subordinate clause.*

Mission 25: Misplaced Modifiers

## ⭐ Step 1: On Guard & Identify Sentences with a Misplaced Modifier

**On Guard.** *Highlight TRUE or FALSE for each question.*

1. <u>Why</u> is a relative pronoun.      TRUE   FALSE

2. Adverbial clauses and phrases modify nouns.      TRUE   FALSE

3. The progressive tense uses <u>to</u> and the simple form of the verb.      TRUE   FALSE

4. A split infinitive is an adverb coming between <u>to</u> and the simple form of the verb.      TRUE   FALSE

5. Indicative mood can be statement of belief.      TRUE   FALSE

**Say each of these words in a sentence.** *Examples are given.*

| | |
|---|---|
| **perception** – opinion | My sister worries about her friends' **perception** too much. |
| **animatedly** – energetically | My little brother demonstrated **animatedly** what happened in the ballgame. |
| **favorable** – positive | Conditions are **favorable** for our picnic tomorrow. |

**Identify sentences with a misplaced modifier.** *Read each sentence. Highlight the sentence if it contains a misplaced modifier.*

1. Reacting to the *Galaxy Life* article, misplaced modifiers had the king upset.

2. The king was worried people would get the wrong idea from the article.

3. Laying more eggs than usual, Cook was thankful for her hens.

4. Cook used the extra eggs to make omelets the king loved.

5. The king was careful not to overeat the omelets in front of the magazine staff.

6. The king didn't know if he should wear a gold man's watch for the interview.

7. Cook served scones to the reporter on a silver plate.

8. She ate the scone she was served slowly.

Mission 25: Misplaced Modifiers

⭐ Step 2: Identify Misplaced Modifiers' Part of Speech

**Reach each sentence that includes an underlined misplaced modifier.**
*Highlight whether the misplaced modifier is an adjective (modifies a noun), adverb (modifies a verb, adjective, or adverb), or dangling participle (-ing verb).*

1. **The king read the article he was handed <u>quickly</u>.**
   adjective          adverb          dangling participle

2. **Before the journalists arrived, the queen requested an <u>elegant</u> woman's hairdo.**
   adjective          adverb          dangling participle

3. **After a coffee spill, the <u>ruined</u> woman's dress caused a delay.**
   adjective          adverb          dangling participle

4. **<u>Hushing the staff</u>, the reporters arrived to a quiet house.**
   adjective          adverb          dangling participle

5. **Cook <u>just</u> gave them a light breakfast.**
   adjective          adverb          dangling participle

6. **She made sure to serve a <u>cold</u> glass of juice.**
   adjective          adverb          dangling participle

7. **<u>Checking the sky for rain</u>, the garden wasn't available for photographs.**
   adjective          adverb          dangling participle

8. **The king <u>nearly</u> gave the reporters eight hours of his time.**
   adjective          adverb          dangling participle


**Activity.** Restate the correctly written sentences for your teacher so that they have a misplaced modifier.

On the way to work, I saw a cute puppy.
He bought a horse called Lightning for his daughter.
The police reported that two banks were robbed this week.
She served ice cream on cones to the children.
Looking to the horizon, the runner spotted a funnel cloud.

Mission 25: Misplaced Modifiers

## ⭐ Step 3: Rewrite Sentences Without a Misplaced Modifier
**Rewrite each sentence so it no longer has a misplaced modifier. Note:** <u>You may have to add words</u>.

1. Constantly making evil plans, the king's daily goal is to defeat the Gremlin.

2. The heavy king's workout gives him the energy he needs for his day.

3. The castle cook served eggs to the king with large rolls.

4. The king said after a long nap he would have a busy day.

5. This misplaced writer has the worst modifiers ever.

6. With no experience, the governor of planet Sentence recently replaced sentence coordinators.

7. It's a hot guardians' mess.

8. Checking the sky for rain, the garden wasn't available for photographs.

**Vocabulary Victory!** Do you remember what these words mean? *Check Step 1 if you need a reminder.*

| perception | I have to change the public's **perception** of me. |
|---|---|
| animatedly | He spoke **animatedly** with the queen about his plan. |
| favorable | He was hopeful that the journalist doing the story would show him in a **favorable** light. |

Mission 25: Misplaced Modifiers

☆ <u>Advanced Guardians Only</u>
**We are asking you a personal favor. Our father is discouraged by his low approval ratings.** Would you write or type him a letter, sharing the positive traits you have seen in him? When you are done writing, please review your letter to make sure there are no misplaced modifiers.

Dear King,

_____

Your Faithful Guardian,

_____

Mission 25: Misplaced Modifiers

**Mission 25: Update**

Dear guardians,

You did a great job identifying and rearranging misplaced modifiers! The king has asked the original sentence coordinators on planet Sentence to come back to work. We are hopeful that we can avoid misplaced modifiers in the future.

But we really want to thank you for the letters of encouragement you sent our father. He loved them. We all need to hear we are doing a good job. Speaking of encouragement, we want to tell you how impressed we are with your work. Please keep it up!

We are sending you the solutions to your mission.

Sincerely,

*Kirk, Luke, and Ellen English*
Guardians of Grammar Galaxy

Mission 25: Misplaced Modifiers

Step 1 Solutions
**On Guard.**

1. <u>Why</u> is a relative pronoun.                                                    TRUE  **FALSE**
2. Adverbial clauses and phrases modify nouns.                                          TRUE  **FALSE**
3. The progressive tense uses <u>to</u> and the simple form of the verb.                TRUE  **FALSE**
4. A split infinitive is an adverb coming between <u>to</u> and the simple form of the verb.  **TRUE**  FALSE
5. Indicative mood can be statement of belief.                                          **TRUE**  FALSE

**Identify sentences with a misplaced modifier.**
1. Reacting to the *Galaxy Life* article, misplaced modifiers had the king upset.
2. The king was worried people would get the wrong idea from the article.
3. Laying more eggs than usual, Cook was thankful for her hens.
4. Cook used the extra eggs to make omelets the king loved.
5. The king was careful not to overeat the omelets in front of the magazine staff.
6. The king didn't know if he should wear a gold man's watch for the interview.
7. Cook served scones to the reporter on a silver plate.
8. She ate the scone she was served slowly.

Step 2 Solutions
1. **The king read the article he was handed <u>quickly</u>.**
   adjective            **adverb**            dangling participle
2. **Before the journalists arrived, the queen requested an <u>elegant</u> woman's hairdo.**
   **adjective**            adverb            dangling participle
3. **After a coffee spill, the <u>ruined</u> woman's dress caused a delay.**
   **adjective**            adverb            dangling participle
4. **<u>Hushing the staff</u>, the reporters arrived to a quiet house.**
   adjective            adverb            **dangling participle**
5. **Cook <u>just</u> gave them a light breakfast.**
   adjective            **adverb**            dangling participle
6. **She made sure to serve a <u>cold</u> glass of juice.**
   **adjective**            adverb            dangling participle
7. **<u>Checking the sky for rain</u>, the garden wasn't available for photographs.**
   adjective            adverb            **dangling participle**
8. **The king <u>nearly</u> gave the reporters eight hours of his time.**
   adjective            **adverb**            dangling participle

**Activity. – answers will vary**
On the way to work, I saw a cute puppy. **On the way to work, a cute puppy appeared.**
He bought a horse called Lightning for his daughter. **He bought a horse for his daughter called Lightning.**
The police reported that two banks were robbed this week. **Two banks were reported robbed by police this week.**
She served ice cream on cones to the children. **She served ice cream to the children on cones.**
Looking to the horizon, the runner spotted a funnel cloud. **Looking to the horizon, a funnel cloud appeared before the runner.**

Step 3 Solutions – answers will vary
1. Constantly making evil plans, the king's daily goal is to defeat the Gremlin.
**The king's daily goal is to defeat the Gremlin, who is constantly making evil plans.**
2. The heavy king's workout gives him the energy he needs for his day.
**The king's heavy workout gives him the energy he needs for his day.**
3. The castle cook served eggs to the king with large rolls.
**The castle cook served eggs with large rolls to the king.**
4. The king said after a long nap he would have a busy day.
**The said that after a busy day, he would often take a long nap.**
5. This misplaced writer has the worst modifiers ever.
**The writer has the worst misplaced modifiers ever.**
6. With no experience, the governor of planet Sentence recently replaced sentence coordinators.
**The governor of planet Sentence recently replaced sentence coordinators with those who have no experience.**
7. It's a hot guardians' mess.
**It's a hot mess for the guardians.**
8. Checking the sky for rain, the garden wasn't available for photographs.
**After checking the sky for rain, the king said the garden wasn't available for photographs.**

**Mission 26: Dashes & Parentheses**

Dear guardians,

Do you continue to write run-on sentences, even though you know that's when two independent sentences are incorrectly connected? If so, you may have heard talk about using dashes and parentheses to include more information in a sentence. While these punctuation marks do serve that purpose, we can't overuse them.

We are on our way to planet Sentence to meet with sentence coordinators (the people who decide how sentences should be put together). That's where you come in. We need your help—particularly with the use of dashes and parentheses.

We are including information from *The Guide to Grammar Galaxy* to help you complete this mission. The king said to thank you in advance.

Sincerely,

*Kirk, Luke, and Ellen English (the king, too)*
Guardians of Grammar Galaxy

| Dashes |
|---|

The dash is a horizontal line used to separate groups of words, unlike the hyphen that is used to separate individual words. Two common dashes are the en dash and the em dash.

**The en dash is shorter (like the size of an *N*).** It is used to show a range.
I have read 15–20 pages.
The war lasted from 1914–1918.

**The em dash is longer (like the size of an *M*).** It is used to replace parentheses, colons, and missing information. The em dash can emphasize words and give writing a more casual feel.
I spend a lot of time in the library (usually in the mystery and biography sections).
I spend a lot of time in the library—usually in the mystery and biography sections.
I love two genres of books: mysteries and biographies.
I love two genres of books—mysteries and biographies.
I checked out a book with the faded title: My——ery Island.

| Parentheses |
|---|

Parentheses ( ) are used to enclose nonessential or extra information. Follow these rules for using parentheses.

**1. Use a complete sentence or dependent clause if parentheses are not needed.**
I rode my bike to the library (after I stopped at my friend's house). - incorrect
After I stopped at my friend's house, I rode my bike to the library. - correct

**2. Use punctuation inside the parentheses if it is a complete sentence or requires different punctuation than the main sentence.**
I heard my mother say she wanted me to mow the lawn (or did I?) before I left.
My mother asked me to mow the lawn before I left. (I wasn't sure I heard that.)

**3. Use commas, colons, and semicolons outside the closing parenthesis.**
When she asked me if I had mowed the lawn (louder this time), I had to admit I had not.

Mission 26: Dashes & Parentheses

## ⭐ Step 1: On Guard & Identify Dashes

**On Guard.** *Highlight the correct answer for each of the following questions.*

1. **Highlight the misplaced modifier in the following sentence:**

   Cook served hot cocoa to the English children in a mug.

2. **Highlight the relative pronoun in the following sentence:**

   The queen gave Ellen the same book that she had read as a child.

3. **Highlight the adverbial clause in the following sentence:**

   The queen and Ellen like to read before they go to bed.

4. **Highlight the progressive tense verb in the following sentence:**

   They have been reading before bed for years.

5. **Highlight the infinitive in the following sentence:**

   They both love to read.




**Say each of these words in a sentence.** *Examples are given.*

| steeled – strengthened | The cashier **steeled** herself to listen to the customer's complaints. |
|---|---|
| splendid – wonderful | My aunt said I did a **splendid** job on my art project. |
| vied – competed | My young cousins **vied** for attention by doing cartwheels. |

Mission 26: Dashes & Parentheses

**Identify dashes**. *Read each sentence. Then highlight whether the punctuation is a hyphen, en dash, or em dash.* **Hint:** <u>Review the information we sent you</u>.

1. The king has been doing press conferences for 20–30 years.
   hyphen         en dash         em dash

2. Cook said she made the king an extra-special dessert.
   hyphen         en dash         em dash

3. The article about the king didn't reveal its source, calling him Mr. G—.
   hyphen         en dash         em dash

4. The 1200-word speech was well received.
   hyphen         en dash         em dash

5. The king didn't think the reporter's question was a problem—until he opened the paper.
   hyphen         en dash         em dash

6. The press conference was scheduled for 6:00–7:00 p.m.
   hyphen         en dash         em dash

7. The king's assistant thought there were 30–40 reporters in attendance.
   hyphen         en dash         em dash

8. After a press conference, the king wants two things—a snack and some sleep.

   hyphen         en dash         em dash

Mission 26: Dashes & Parentheses

## ⭐ Step 2: Determine Whether Parentheses Are Used Correctly

**Read each sentence.** *Using the guidelines we sent you for parentheses, highlight whether the sentence is written correctly or incorrectly.*

1. The king was surprised (actually shocked!) when he saw the news headline.
   correct        incorrect

2. Where are you going (and so late at night?)?
   correct        incorrect

3. The king couldn't sleep (worrying about his approval ratings,) so he got up.
   correct        incorrect

4. Later the king asked the Galactic Bureau of Intelligence (GBI) to check out the reporter.
   correct        incorrect

5. One of the agents (the king's good friend) got back to him right away.
   correct        incorrect

6. He said he suspected the reporter was a plant (The Gremlin had sent him).
   correct        incorrect

7. He was asked for his credentials (proof he was a journalist;) he claimed he left his ID at home.
   correct        incorrect

8. The GBI doesn't know his current whereabouts. (He hasn't been seen since the press conference.)
   correct        incorrect

**Activity.** *In your other reading today, track how many hyphens, en dashes, and em dashes you find. Which is used most often?*

Mission 26: Dashes & Parentheses

## ⭐ Step 3: Add Dashes and Parentheses to Sentences

**Read each sentence.** *Add dashes and parentheses where needed to make sentences correct.* **Note:** *You may need to add other punctuation as well.*

1. The State of the Galaxy speech also known as the SOG is watched by most citizens of the galaxy.

2. The queen always watches the SOG with popcorn but she can't watch the critics.

3. The Prime Minister leader of the government gives a short speech after the king finishes.

4. The queen couldn't remember how long he had been Prime Minister maybe 5 7 years?

5. She expected her husband to arrive home from 9 9:30 p.m.

6. "I thought he did a splendid I have to go! He's home."

7. "Were you watching?" He knew she was, but he asked anyway.

8. "I have two favorite parts of the SOG the applause when it's over and coming home to you," the king said.


**Vocabulary Victory!** Do you remember what these words mean? *Check Step 1 if you need a reminder.*

| steeled | He **steeled** himself to meet with the press afterward. |
|---|---|
| splendid | I think they're doing a **splendid** job. |
| vied | The other reporters **vied** for the chance to ask the next question. |

Mission 26: Dashes & Parentheses

## ⭐ Advanced Guardians Only
**Write or type your own State of the Galaxy address.** How do you think the galaxy is doing with reading, spelling, vocabulary, and grammar so far this year? Be sure to use dashes and parentheses where appropriate.

Mission 26: Dashes & Parentheses

**Mission 26: Update**

Dear guardians,

You are the best! Your completed missions were very helpful to us as we coached the sentence coordinators. The other good news is Father was able to stop the overuse of dashes and parentheses (so crisis avoided).

Your State of the Galaxy addresses were encouraging. We have more work to do, but we are making progress.

As you check the solutions to your mission, you'll see that there is more than one right way to use these punctuation marks. (We love that.)

Sincerely,

*Kirk, Luke, and Ellen English*
Guardians of Grammar Galaxy

P.S. You're ready to take the Grammar Challenge! You may want to review what you've learned in this unit first. But we know you've got this!

Mission 26: Dashes & Parentheses

Step 1 Solutions

**On Guard.**

1. **Highlight the misplaced modifier in the following sentence:**
   Cook served hot cocoa to the English children ==in a mug==.
2. **Highlight the relative pronoun in the following sentence:**
   The queen gave Ellen the same book ==that== she had read as a child.
3. **Highlight the adverbial clause in the following sentence:**
   The queen and Ellen like to read ==before they go to bed==.
4. **Highlight the progressive tense verb in the following sentence:**
   They ==have been reading== before bed for years.
5. **Highlight the infinitive in the following sentence:**
   They both love ==to read==.

**Identify dashes.**

1. The king has been doing press conferences for 20–30 years.
   hyphen    ==en dash==    em dash
2. Cook said she made the king an extra-special dessert.
   ==hyphen==    en dash    em dash
3. The article about the king didn't reveal its source, calling him Mr. G—.
   hyphen    en dash    ==em dash==
4. The 1200-word speech was well received.
   ==hyphen==    en dash    em dash
5. The king didn't think the reporter's question was a problem—until he opened the paper.
   hyphen    en dash    ==em dash==
6. The press conference was scheduled for 6:00–7:00 p.m.
   hyphen    ==en dash==    em dash
7. The king's assistant thought there were 30–40 reporters in attendance.
   hyphen    ==en dash==    em dash
8. After a press conference, the king wants two things—a snack and some sleep.
   hyphen    en dash    ==em dash==

Step 2 Solutions

1. The king was surprised (actually shocked!) when he saw the news headline.
   ==correct==    incorrect
2. Where are you going (and so late at night?)?
   correct    ==incorrect==
3. The king couldn't sleep (worrying about his approval ratings,) so he got up.
   correct    ==incorrect==
4. Later the king asked the Galactic Bureau of Intelligence (GBI) to check out the reporter.
   ==correct==    incorrect
5. One of the agents (the king's good friend) got back to him right away.
   ==correct==    incorrect
6. He said he suspected the reporter was a plant (The Gremlin had sent him).
   correct    ==incorrect==
7. He was asked for his credentials (proof he was a journalist;) he claimed he left his ID at home.
   correct    ==incorrect==
8. The GBI doesn't know his current whereabouts. (He hasn't been seen since the press conference.)
   ==correct==    incorrect

Step 3 Solutions

1. The State of the Galaxy speech (also known as the SOG) is watched by most citizens of the galaxy.
2. The queen always watches the SOG with popcorn—but she can't watch the critics. **Parentheses around but she can't watch the critics is also correct.**
3. The Prime Minister (leader of the government) gives a short speech after the king finishes.
4. The queen couldn't remember how long he had been Prime Minister (maybe 5–7 years?). **An em dash before *maybe* is also correct.**
5. She expected her husband to arrive home from 9–9:30 p.m.
6. "I thought he did a splendid—I have to go! He's home."
7. "Were you watching?" (He knew she was, but he asked anyway.)
8. "I have two favorite parts of the SOG—the applause when it's over and coming home to you," the king said.

# Grammar Challenge I

**Carefully read all the possible answers** and then highlight the letter for the **one** best answer.

1. **An en dash is used to:**
    a. show a range
    b. replace parentheses
    c. connect words
2. **Misplaced modifiers can be:**
    a. adjectives
    b. adverbs
    c. both a and b
3. **Relative pronouns begin:**
    a. adverbial clauses
    b. adjective clauses
    c. infinitives
4. **The conjunction <u>wherever</u> is often used in:**
    a. the progressive tense
    b. adverbial phrases
    c. adverbial clauses
5. **How many progressive tenses are there?**
    a. four
    b. five
    c. six
6. **Infinitives most commonly begin with the word:**
    a. to
    b. be
    c. will

7. **Imperative mood:**
   a. asks a question
   b. makes a statement of fact or belief
   c. issues a command
8. **In diagramming, subject and predicate go on:**
   a. the vertical line.
   b. the horizontal line.
   c. the slanted line.
9. **The subjunctive mood uses which form of the verb?**
   a. first person
   b. second person
   c. third person
10. **Infinitives can be used as:**
    a. nouns
    b. verbs
    c. neither a nor b

Number Correct:_____/10

## ⭐ Advanced Guardian Vocabulary Challenge

For an extra challenge, highlight the word that best fits each blank.

1. My friends and I _____ to catch candy at the parade.
   intoned          vied          lauded

2. We shouldn't worry about others' _____ of us.
   perception       endeavor      concession

3. I can tell when my mother is upset because she speaks _____.
   accessible       depicted      curtly

4. My father doesn't like it when other cars _____ our progress.
   ire              impede        usurp

5. Every Saturday, my mother has cleaning on the _____.
   vexation         amenable      agenda

6. Most days I have _____ to get my chores done.
   bustled          irked         splendid

7. My little brothers speaks _____ about sports.
   disconcerted     animatedly    shady

8. My small bedroom is not exactly _____.
   amenable         depicted      palatial

9. I _____ myself to go out into the cold.
   favorable        steeled       vexation

Number Correct: _____/9

## Grammar Challenge 1 Answers
1.a; 2.c; 3.b; 4.c; 5.c; 6.a; 7.c; 8.b; 9.c; 10.a

**If you got 9 or more correct, congratulations!** You've earned your Grammar star. You may add it to your Grammar Guardian bookmark. You are ready for an adventure in composition and speaking.

**If you did not get 9 or more correct, don't worry.** You have another chance. You may want to review the information from each chapter you've read so far. Then take the Grammar Challenge 2. Remember to **choose the <u>one</u> best answer**.

## Advanced Guardian Vocabulary Challenge Answers
1. vied
2. perception
3. curtly
4. impede
5. agenda
6. bustled
7. animatedly
8. palatial
9. steeled

# Grammar Challenge 2

*Carefully read all the possible answers* and then highlight the letter for the **one** best answer.

1. **I love two genres of books mysteries and biographies.**
   Which is the correct version of the sentence above?
   a. I love two genres of books: mysteries and biographies.
   b. I love two genres of books—mysteries and biographies.
   c. Both a and b are correct.

2. **Rotting in the basement, my brother brought up a case of apples.**
   Which is the correct version of the sentence above?
   a. My brother, rotting in the basement, brought up a case of apples.
   b. My brother brought up a case of apples that he found rotting in the basement.
   c. Both a and be are correct.

3. **I am enjoying the book that is the second in a series.**
   Which word in the sentence above is the relative pronoun?
   a. I
   b. that
   c. second

4. **I like reading to pass the time.**
   What part of speech is the infinitive in this sentence?
   a. noun
   b. adjective
   c. adverb

5. **By 3:00 today, she will have been playing the game for four hours.**
   What is the tense of the verb in the sentence?
   a. future
   b. future perfect
   c. future perfect progressive

6. Which of these is a split infinitive?
   a. to write carefully
   b. to carefully write
   c. neither a nor b

7. Which sentence is written in the correct subjunctive mood?
   a. If I was a millionaire, I'd buy a sports care.
   b. I wish I was a millionaire.
   c. If I were a millionaire, I'd travel the world.

8. How many slanted lines would be in the diagram of the sentence <u>Old dogs learn new tricks.</u>?
   a. two
   b. three
   c. four

9. What is the grammatical mood of the sentence <u>What in the world are you doing?</u>
   a. conditional
   b. interrogative
   c. indicative

10. I can read <u>in the car</u>.
    What is the underlined part of the sentence?
    a. adverbial phrase
    b. adverbial clause
    c. adjective clause

Number Correct:_____/10

Grammar Challenge

Grammar Challenge 2 Answers
1.c; 2.b; 3.b; 4.c; 5.c; 6.b; 7.c; 8.a; 9.b; 10.a

**If you got 9 or more correct, congratulations!** You've earned your Grammar star. You may add a star to your bookmark. You are now ready for an adventure in composition and speaking.

**If you did not get 9 or more correct, don't worry.** Review the questions you missed. You may want to get more practice using the resources at GrammarGalaxyBooks.com/BlueStar for grammar. Your teacher can ask you other questions like the ones you missed and if you get them correct, you'll have earned your Grammar star and can move on to an adventure in composition and speaking.

# Unit IV: Adventures in Composition & Speaking

# OFFICIAL GUARDIAN MAIL

**Mission 27: Parallel Structure**

Dear guardian friends,

You have no doubt heard about the gymnast who was injured at the Galaxy Gymnastic Championships. We don't have an update for you on his condition yet. But we do have a problem that requires your help.

Parallel sentence structure has nothing to do with parallel bars in gymnastics. However, it has been forbidden anyway. The king is working to change that. Your mission now is to complete the On Guard review questions, identify unparallel structure, and then we want you to practice writing with parallel structure. ← This isn't parallel, if you didn't notice.

Using your completed missions, we will be helping the sentence coordinators on planet Sentence restore parallel structure. Thank you for your prompt attention.

Sincerely,

*Kirk, Luke, and Ellen English*
Guardians of Grammar Galaxy

## ★ Step 1: On Guard & Identify Unparallel Structure

**On Guard.** *Highlight the correct answer for each question.*

1. Parentheses are used to enclose _____ information.
   essential            nonessential            dependent

2. Dangling participles are _____.
   -ing verbs           nouns                   prepositions

3. Relative pronouns begin _____.
   phrases              adjective clauses       sentences

4. Phrases that communicate where, when, how, or why are _____.
   noun                 adjective               adverbial

5. Progressive tense is used to show that a verb's action is _____.
   complete             ongoing                 future

**Say each of these words in a sentence.** *Examples are given.*

| sacrifice – give up | My parents don't want to **sacrifice** quality for a good deal. |
|---|---|
| subdued – quiet | The crowd was **subdued** after the other team scored three runs. |
| stay – stop | The court ordered a **stay** of business operation until the lawsuit was settled. |

Mission 27: Parallel Structure

**Identify unparallel structure**. *Read each sentence. If the structure of the sentence is not parallel, highlight the sentence.*

1. Ellen's favorite gymnastic events are Balance Beam, Vault, and her favorite is the floor exercise.

2. Luke's favorite gymnastic events are the Still Rings, the Pommel Horse, and he loves the Vault.

3. Kirk is most interested in the history, the athletes, and ceremony of gymnastics.

4. The queen's favorite female gymnasts are Simone Biles, Nadia Comaneci, and Kerri Strug.

5. Wrist fractures, ligament tears, and athletes with damage to cartilage are common injures in gymnastics.

6. Kirk looked up the high school sports that cause the most injuries and they are basketball, football, and soccer.

7. Ellen wants to participate in a sport that challenges her, keeps her fit, and she wants to make friends.

8. The king wants Ellen to be in a sport that promotes fitness, sportsmanship, and is inexpensive.

Mission 27: Parallel Structure

## ⭐ Step 2: Highlight Unparallel Sentence Structure

**Read each sentence that lacks parallel structure.** *Highlight the part of the sentence that does not have the same grammatical structure as the rest of the sentence.*

1. The most popular sports for high school boys are basketball, all of the events that make up track and field, and baseball.

2. Cross country, swimming, and the track and field events are supposed to be the safest sports for boys.

3. Boys' sports that increased in popularity last year are track and field, soccer, wrestling, tennis, and boys' volleyball.

4. Football with 11 players has decreased in popularity due to shifts to smaller teams, to an increase in 8-player football, and due to safety concerns.

5. Basketball is the most popular, American, for high school girls sport.

6. Swimming is supposed to be the safest sport for girls, cross country is supposed to be the second safest, and finally, tennis.

7. Girls' sports with the greatest increase in popularity are volleyball, soccer, and the sport of lacrosse.

8. Kids who participate in sports are less likely to be obese, to have chronic illness, and more likely to graduate from high school.

**Activity.** *Intentionally speak without using parallel structure during a family meal. Does anyone notice?*

Mission 27: Parallel Structure

## ⭐ Step 3: Rewrite Sentences Using Parallel Structure
**Read each sentence from Steps 1 and 2.** *Write to finish the sentence correctly, being careful to use parallel structure.* **Note:** *Check the sentences from Steps 1 and 2 before writing.*

1. Ellen's favorite gymnastic events are Balance Beam, Vault, and
_____.

2. Luke's favorite gymnastic events are the Still Rings, the Pommel Horse, and
_____.

3. Kirk is most interested in the history, the athletes, and
_____.

4. Wrist fractures, ligament tears, and _____
are common injuries in gymnastics.

5. Ellen wants to participate in a sport that challenges her, keeps her fit, and
_____.

6. The king wants Ellen to be in a sport that promotes fitness,
_____.

7. Girls' sports with the greatest increase in popularity are volleyball, soccer, and _____.

8. Kids who participate in sports are less likely to be obese,
_____
_____.


**Vocabulary Victory!** Do you remember what these words mean? *Check Step 1 if you need a reminder.*

| sacrifice | The queen explained that she would have to **sacrifice** another activity first. |
|---|---|
| subdued | The accident had the audience **subdued** for the rest of the competition. |
| stay | The head of the Galaxy Gymnastics Association is calling for an immediate **stay** on parallel bars competition. |

Mission 27: Parallel Structure

☆ Advanced Guardians Only
**Write three reasons you'd like to participate in a sport or activity.** *Be sure to use parallel structure.*

_____
_____
_____
_____
_____
_____
_____

**Mission 27: Update**

Dear guardians,

We have good news to report about the injured gymnast. He does have a bone fracture, but it hasn't affected his movement. Doctors believe he will recover and will be able to compete again.

The other good news is we can use parallel structure. Father explained that it's not only safe but makes what we write and say easier to understand.

We are interested in a lot of sports and activities after reading your advanced mission assignments. Thanks for those. Ellen is happy to report that she has permission to participate in gymnastics.

Before you go to practice the sport or activity of your choice, please review the solutions to this mission.

Sincerely,

*Kirk, Luke, and Ellen English*
Guardians of Grammar Galaxy

Mission 27: Parallel Structure

Step 1 Solutions
**On Guard.**
1. Parentheses are used to enclose _____ information.
   essential                    nonessential                    dependent
2. Dangling participles are _____.
   -ing verbs                   nouns                           prepositions
3. Relative pronouns begin _____.
   phrases                      adjective clauses               sentences
4. Phrases that communicate where, when, how, or why are _____.
   noun                         adjective                       adverbial
5. Progressive tense is used to show that a verb's action is _____.
   complete                     ongoing                         future

**Identify unparallel structure.**

1. Ellen's favorite gymnastic events are Balance Beam, Vault, and her favorite is the floor exercise.

2. Luke's favorite gymnastic events are the Still Rings, the Pommel Horse, and he loves the Vault.

3. Kirk is most interested in the history, the athletes, and ceremony of gymnastics.

4. The queen's favorite female gymnasts are Simone Biles, Nadia Comaneci, and Kerri Strug.

5. Wrist fractures, ligament tears, and athletes with damage to cartilage are common injuries in gymnastics.

6. Kirk looked up the high school sports that cause the most injuries and they are basketball, football, and soccer.

7. Ellen wants to participate in a sport that challenges her, keeps her fit, and she wants to make friends.

8. The king wants Ellen to be in a sport that promotes fitness, sportsmanship, and is inexpensive.

Step 2 Solutions

1. The most popular sports for high school boys are basketball, all of the events that make up track and field, and baseball.

2. Cross country, swimming, and the track and field events are supposed to be the safest sports for boys.

3. Boys' sports that increased in popularity last year are track and field, soccer, wrestling, tennis, and boys' volleyball. – **track and field may also be highlighted.**

4. Football with 11 players has decreased in popularity due to shifts to smaller teams, to an increase in 8-player football, and due to safety concerns.

5. Basketball is the most popular, American, for high school girls sport.

6. Swimming is supposed to be the safest sport for girls, cross country is supposed to be the second safest, and finally, tennis.

7. Girls' sports with the greatest increase in popularity are volleyball, soccer, and the sport of lacrosse.

8. Kids who participate in sports are less likely to be obese, to have chronic illness, and more likely to graduate from high school.

Step 3 Solutions
1. Ellen's favorite gymnastic events are Balance Beam, Vault, and Floor Exercise.
2. Luke's favorite gymnastic events are the Still Rings, the Pommel Horse, and Vault.
3. Kirk is most interested in the history, the athletes, and the ceremony of gymnastics.
4. Wrist fractures, ligament tears, and cartilage damage are common injures in gymnastics.
5. Ellen wants to participate in a sport that challenges her, keeps her fit, and helps her make friends.
6. The king wants Ellen to be in a sport that promotes fitness, teaches sportsmanship, and is inexpensive.
7. Girls' sports with the greatest increase in popularity are volleyball, soccer, and lacrosse.
8. Kids who participate in sports are less likely to be obese, less likely to have chronic illness, and more likely to graduate from high school.

**Mission 28: Morning Pages**

Dear guardians,

Our cook taught us her practice of writing morning pages. Each day, usually in the morning, she writes three pages in her journal. She writes by hand, doesn't show them to anyone, and writes about anything.

She encouraged us to try writing morning pages, too. And believe it or not, we like it! Our handwriting is faster. We can think through any worries or problems we have. And we come up with great writing ideas.

We would like you to try it! You'll need a journal because you'll complete your mission steps in it. Also, find a pen that you like.

The only part of this mission we need to see are your On Guard questions and what you think of morning pages. We hope you enjoy writing them as much as we do.

Sincerely,

*Kirk, Luke, and Ellen English*
Guardians of Grammar Galaxy

## ⭐ Step 1: On Guard & Write a Morning Pages Task List

**On Guard.** *Highlight the correct answer for each question.*

1. **Parallel structure is also known as:**
   clauses      modifiers      parallelism

2. **The punctuation mark used to separate groups of words is the:**
   dash      hyphen      apostrophe

3. **Modifiers separated from the word they describe are called:**
   progressive      infinitive      misplaced

4. **The word <u>that</u> at the beginning of an adjective clause is a _____ pronoun.**
   progressive      relative      misplaced

5. **Adverbial clauses are _____ clauses.**
   subjective      independent      dependent

**Say each of these words in a sentence.** *Examples are given.*

| **pastime** – hobby | Coin collecting is my uncle's **pastime**. |
|---|---|
| **consistently** – regularly | My mother says cleaning should be done **consistently**. |
| **consciousness** – awareness | The fan who was hit by a baseball briefly lost **consciousness**. |

Mission 28: Morning Pages

**Write a morning pages task list.** Using your journal and a favorite pen, write three pages of tasks you need or would like to do. Some ideas are chores to complete, school assignments to finish, books to read, movies to watch, places to visit, and games to play.

Mission 28: Morning Pages

⭐ Step 2: Write Morning Pages About a Problem
**Write three morning pages in your journal about something that is bothering you.** You might write about a school subject that's a struggle, a relationship conflict that's bothering you, or a fear you have. If you still have space to write after describing the problem and your feelings, write about some potential solutions. Include new ways of thinking about the problem.

**Activity.** *Find and read something you wrote when you were younger—a journal if you have one. Ask your parent to help you. How have you changed as a person and as a writer? Do you think you would enjoy reading today's morning pages in the future?*

☆ Step 3: Write Morning Pages About Writing

**Sometimes you don't know what to write about in your morning pages.** *In that case, write three pages about how you feel about morning pages or writing in general. That's your journal mission for today.*

**Vocabulary Victory!** Do you remember what these words mean? *Check Step 1 if you need a reminder.*

| pastime | She was excited to talk about her new **pastime**. |
|---|---|
| consistently | "Do you keep a journal?" she asked the queen. "Not **consistently**," the queen admitted. |
| consciousness | It's stream-of-**consciousness** writing. |

☆ Advanced Guardians Only

**Write three morning pages of your ideas for a book you'd like to write one day.** It can be a fiction or nonfiction book. If you aren't interested in writing a book, write three morning pages about why you aren't.

# OFFICIAL GUARDIAN MAIL

**Mission 28: Update**

Dear guardians,

We've heard from some of you about morning pages. Most of you weren't sure about them at first but started to enjoy writing them. Some of you asked if you have to continue. The answer is no. But if you enjoy it, we recommend that you keep up the habit. If you don't, try writing just one page a day. That might make a difference.

We are including the On Guard solutions for this mission. Whether you continue morning pages or not, we want you to write consistently to keep the galaxy strong.

Sincerely,

*Kirk, Luke, and Ellen English*
Guardians of Grammar Galaxy

Step 1 Solutions

**On Guard.**
1. **Parallel structure is also known as:**
   clauses modifiers **parallelism**
2. **The punctuation mark used to separate groups of words is the:**
   **dash** hyphen apostrophe
3. **Modifiers separated from the word they describe are called:**
   progressive infinitive **misplaced**
4. **The word <u>that</u> at the beginning of an adjective clause is a _____ pronoun.**
   progressive **relative** misplaced
5. **Adverbial clauses are _____ clauses.**
   subjective independent **dependent**

**Mission 29: Passive Voice**

Dear guardians,

We have been given instructions for a new mission. The sentence coordinators have been told that passive voice will create peace. But that's not true. Passive voice should be used infrequently, but now we are overusing it. Our father says we are all being made inactive as a result.

You are being sent a mission to correct the problem. Sentence coordinators will be taught using your completed missions.

Gratefully,

*Kirk, Luke, and Ellen English*
Guardians of Grammar Galaxy

P.S. You will be supplied with information on the next page.

## Passive Voice

**Passive voice** is when the subject of a sentence is being acted upon. A sentence is in passive voice when a form of *be* (is, am, are, was, were, being, been) is paired with the past participle of the verb (i.e., the present or past perfect verb often ending in -ed).

The passive agent (that acts on the subject) may be added to the sentence with the word *by*.

Most telescopes **are manufactured** in China and Taiwan.
A new space program will **be launched** in two years.
Pluto **was discovered by Clyde Tombaugh**. (passive agent)

Verbs that cannot have direct objects are never in passive voice (e.g., arrive, come, die, go, live, sleep).

**Active voice** emphasizes the subject as the acting agent.

China and Taiwan **manufacture** the most telescopes.
The country **will launch** a new space program in two years.
Clyde Tombaugh **discovered** Pluto.

**Use passive voice sparingly.** Active voice makes sentences easier to understand.

Mission 29: Passive Voice

## ⭐ Step 1: On Guard & Identify Sentences in Passive Voice
**On Guard.** *Highlight the best answer for each question.*

1. **Morning pages should be written:**
   daily                in the morning            with a keyboard

2. **Luke likes to eat apples, bananas, and _____.**
   quickly              grapes                    in the morning

3. **Planet English is the home of Galaxy Aeronautics and Space Administration __ GASA __.**
   —   —              - -                        ( )

4. **Groggy in the morning, _____ better later in the day.**
   Luke is              writing is                morning pages are

5. **Morning pages are easier to write after eating chocolate chip banana muffins____which are the queen's favorite.**
   –                    ,                         no punctuation needed


**Say each of these words in a sentence.** *Examples are given.*

| disturbing – worrying | My mother finds TV news **disturbing**. |
|---|---|
| disregarded – ignored | Many library fine notices are **disregarded**. |
| diminished – reduced | The medicine the doctor gave me **diminished** the swelling. |

Mission 29: Passive Voice

**Identify sentences in passive voice.** *Read each sentence. Highlight the sentence if it is written in passive voice.*

1. The king wanted his family to exercise with him.

2. Kirk was asked to stop what he was doing and go to the gym.

3. Luke was being entertained by Comet.

4. Ellen had been invited to a party by friends.

5. But the family did arrive at the gym to workout.

6. They were expected to do the workout the king had planned.

7. The queen tried to make a joke about lifting weights.

8. The royal family was delayed in finishing their workout.

Mission 29: Passive Voice

### ⭐ Step 2: Identify the Subject and Passive Agent
**Read each sentence written in passive voice.** <u>Underline</u> *the simple subject of the sentence (without articles or adjectives). If there is a simple passive agent in the sentence,* ==highlight== *it. The first one is done for you.* **Note:** <u>The subject may be a pronoun.</u>

Most <u>books</u> are read by young ==adults==.

1. Sentence <u>coordinators</u> were misled by the ==Gremlin==.

2. <u>They</u> were taught that passive voice equals peace.

3. <u>Protesters</u> were given signs to carry.

4. <u>They</u> had been fooled by the ==Gremlin==.

5. <u>Protesters</u> were asked to leave by ==Grammar Patrol==.

6. But <u>signs</u> were left behind.

7. <u>Sentences</u> were still being written in passive voice.

8. <u>Guardians</u> of the galaxy were given a new mission by ==Kirk==, ==Luke==, and ==Ellen==.

**Activity.** *Find dumbbells or canned goods to do a bench press exercise (lie on your back and push the weights into the air by extending your arms). You may substitute a pushup. Roll a die or use a random number generator for numbers 1-6. If the sentence number you roll is in active voice, you must do that number of sets of 8 bench press or pushup repetitions. If the sentence number you roll is in passive voice, you do not have to do any sets, but you must roll again.*

1. The king was ignored by his family at first.
2. But exercise is important.
3. The king wants his children to be fit.
4. The children did try the bench press.
5. The queen was pressured to participate by the king.
6. The workout was interrupted by a mission.

Mission 29: Passive Voice

## ⭐ Step 3: Rewrite Sentences in Active Voice

**Read each sentence.** *Rewrite what we said so it is in active voice, using the lines below.* **Note:** *Try using the passive agent as the subject.*

1. I was being taught a lot about a new coding language.
   _____
   _____

2. I was invited to a party by my friends.
   _____
   _____

3. The invitation is being sent to me right now.
   _____
   _____

4. I'm being entertained by Comet.
   _____
   _____

5. I'll be turned into a beast by the weight machine.
   _____
   _____

6. I was wiped out by the bench press.
   _____
   _____

7. I am being made late by this workout.
   _____
   _____

8. How long will we be worked out by you?
   _____
   _____

**Vocabulary Victory!** Do you remember what these words mean? *Check Step 1 if you need a reminder.*

| disturbing | He had heard **disturbing** things about the effects of lack of exercise in children. |
|---|---|
| disregarded | The king **disregarded** her argument and asked her to help round up the three kids. |
| diminished | The king's enthusiasm wasn't **diminished** by his family's reaction. |

☆ Advanced Guardians Only

**Write three reasons exercise is important in passive voice. Then rewrite the three reasons in active voice. Note:** *Be sure to write complete sentences with a subject and verb.* Which voice is more convincing?

**Three reasons exercise is important (passive voice).**

1. _____
2. _____
3. _____

**Three reasons exercise is important (active voice).**

1. _____
2. _____
3. _____

**Mission 29: Update**

Dear friends,

    We traveled to planet Sentence via the shuttle. (That sounds so much better than saying we were transported to planet Sentence by the shuttle.) When we arrived, we were able to use your completed missions to help the sentence coordinators use active voice. Grammar Patrol broke up the "Passives Voices for Peace" protests, so you should notice that you're using active voice more often.

    Your reasons for exercising (especially the ones you wrote in active voice) were so convincing that we want to work out with our father regularly. He is thrilled.

    Please check your mission solutions with the answers we are sending you.

Sincerely,

*Kirk, Luke, and Ellen English*
Guardians of Grammar Galaxy

Mission 29: Passive Voice

Step 1 Solutions
**On Guard.**
1. **Morning pages should be written:**
   daily                    in the morning              with a keyboard
2. **Luke likes to eat apples, bananas, and _____.**
   quickly                  grapes                      in the morning
3. **Planet English is the home of Galaxy Aeronautics and Space Administration __ GASA __.**
   — —                     - -                         ( )
4. **Groggy in the morning, _____ better later in the day.**
   Luke is                  writing is                  morning pages are
5. **Morning pages are easier to write after eating chocolate chip banana muffins____which are the queen's favorite.**
   -                        ,                           no punctuation needed

**Identify sentences in passive voice.**
1. The king wanted his family to exercise with him.
2. Kirk was asked to stop what he was doing and go to the gym.
3. Luke was being entertained by Comet.
4. Ellen had been invited to a party by friends.
5. But the family did arrive at the gym to workout.
6. They were expected to do the workout the king had planned.
7. The queen tried to make a joke about lifting weights.
8. The royal family was delayed in finishing their workout.

Step 2 Solutions
1. Sentence coordinators were misled by the Gremlin.
2. They were taught that passive voice equals peace.
3. Protesters were given signs to carry.
4. They had been fooled by the Gremlin.
5. Protesters were asked to leave by Grammar Patrol.
6. But signs were left behind.
7. Sentences were still being written in passive voice.
8. Guardians of the galaxy were given a new mission by Kirk, Luke, and Ellen.

**Activity.**
1. The king was ignored by his family at first. – no sets; roll again
2. But exercise is important. – 2 sets
3. The king wants his children to be fit. – 3 sets
4. The children did try the bench press. – 4 sets
5. The queen was pressured to participate by the king. – no sets; roll again
6. The workout was interrupted by a mission. – no sets; roll again

Step 3 Solutions – answers may vary
1. I was being taught a lot about a new coding language.
I was learning a lot about a new coding language.
2. I was invited to a party by my friends.
My friends invited me to a party.
3. The invitation is being sent to me right now.
They are sending me the invitation right now.
4. I'm being entertained by Comet.
Comet is entertaining me.
5. I'll be turned into a beast by the weight machine.
The weight machine will turn me into a beast.
6. I was wiped out by the bench press.
The bench press wiped me out.
7. I am being made late by this workout.
This workout is making me late.
8. How long will we be worked out by you?
How long will you work us out?

**Mission 30: Profile Essays**

Dear guardians,

*Women's Universe* is asking for nominations of women who make a difference in the universe. Ellen is going to nominate our cook by writing a profile essay. After learning how to write these essays, Ellen thought it would be a great idea for all the guardians to write them.

Your mission is to write a profile essay of someone who makes a difference in your community. We look forward to reading them!

Sincerely,

*Kirk, Luke, and Ellen English*
Guardians of Grammar Galaxy

Mission 30: Profile Essays

## ⭐ Step 1: On Guard & Prepare to Write a Profile Essay

**On Guard.** *Highlight TRUE or FALSE for each statement.*

1. Passive voice includes a form of the word *be* and a past participle.     TRUE    FALSE

2. Morning pages are only valuable if you're an author.     TRUE    FALSE

3. Parallel structure means using the same form of punctuation throughout a sentence.     TRUE    FALSE

4. Parentheses are used to enclose nonessential information.     TRUE    FALSE

5. You can correct a misplaced modifier by moving it closer to the word it modifies.     TRUE    FALSE


**Say each of these words in a sentence.** *Examples are given.*

| | |
|---|---|
| **influence** – authority | Teachers have a lot of **influence** in their students' lives. |
| **legitimate** – real | The news story about UFOs wasn't **legitimate**. |
| **affirmation** – support | My friend needs a lot of **affirmation** as he recovers from his injury. |

**Prepare to write a profile essay.** *Read at least two profile essays about people who have made a difference in their communities. Find links to essays at GrammarGalaxyBooks.com/BlueStar. Note below how the essays are organized and the parts that were most interesting to you and why.*

*Then prepare to interview the person you are profiling. On the next pages, you'll find space to collect biographical information about your subject and write questions to ask during the interview. Be sure to include questions about positive influences, challenges, and successes in childhood, education, career, hobbies, community service, and family life. Also be sure to ask about your subject's dreams for the future. Schedule the interview and take notes in the blanks provided. Find a printable form at GrammarGalaxyBooks.com/BlueStar.*

How are the essays organized? List the main topics described in each essay.




Which parts of the essays were most interesting to you? Why?

Mission 30: Profile Essays

Interview Date/Time_____ Subject Name_____
Date and Place of Birth_____
Places Lived_____
Schools Attended_____
Jobs/Positions Held_____
Family Members_____
Hobbies_____
Community Service_____
Awards/Recognition_____

1._____
_____

2._____
_____

3._____
_____

4._____
_____

5._____
_____

6._____
_____

7._____
_____

8._____
_____

9._____
_____

10._____
_____

11._____
_____

12._____
_____

13._____
_____

14._____
_____

15._____
_____

16._____
_____

☆ Step 2: Outline Your Essay

**After you complete your interview, create an outline for your essay.** *First, decide if you will organize your essay chronologically or by topic. Write the time periods or topics in the outline below. Use your interview notes to add the details under A, B, and C for each time period/topic. Include quotes if they add to the story.*

**Introduction (the most interesting, biggest problem, greatest accomplishment)**


**I. Time period/topic**_____
    A.

    B.

    C.

**II. Time period/topic**_____
    A.

    B.

    C.

**III. Time period/topic**_____
    A.

    B.

    C.

**Conclusion (summarize your view, mention topic of the introduction)**


**Activity.** *Spend time with the person you are profiling, if possible. Observe them in their job, community work, hobbies, or family.*

## ⭐ Step 3: Write the Profile Essay

**Using your outline from Step 2, type a first draft of your profile essay.** *You should have at least five paragraphs written when you are done.* **Note:** *First drafts aren't perfect.*

**Vocabulary Victory!** Do you remember what these words mean? *Check Step 1 if you need a reminder.*

| influence | If she nominated her, the queen worried that Cook would be selected because of her royal **influence**. |
|---|---|
| legitimate | Cook wouldn't see it as a **legitimate** honor. |
| affirmation | Cook would appreciate words of **affirmation** from Ellen even more than from the queen. |

## ⭐ Advanced Guardians Only

**Edit your profile essay.** *Correct spelling and grammar errors. Add more descriptive language and vary sentence starters. Ask someone to read your essay and make suggestions for improvements. Finally, ask the person you profiled to read it. Make any changes they request.*

**OFFICIAL GUARDIAN MAIL**

**Mission 30: Update**

Dear guardian friends,

Ellen interviewed Cook, spent time with her at the soup kitchen, and wrote a first draft of a profile essay about her. After our mother edited the essay, Ellen gave it to Cook to read. Cook cried, which doesn't make sense to us boys. But Ellen said they were happy tears. She submitted the profile essay to *Women's Universe,* and now we wait.

We know Cook makes a big difference in her community, but many of the people you interviewed do, too. They all deserve an award! Please consider this letter an award for learning to write excellent profile essays.

We are including the solutions to the On Guard questions for your mission.

Sincerely,

*Kirk, Luke, and Ellen English*
Guardians of Grammar Galaxy

Mission 30: Profile Essays

Step 1 Solutions
**On Guard.**
1. Passive voice includes a form of the word *be* and a past participle. — **TRUE** FALSE
2. Morning pages are only valuable if you're an author. — TRUE **FALSE**
3. Parallel structure means using the same form of punctuation throughout a sentence. — TRUE **FALSE**
4. Parentheses are used to enclose nonessential information. — **TRUE** FALSE
5. You can correct a misplaced modifier by moving it closer to the word it modifies. — **TRUE** FALSE

**Mission 31: Writing Summaries**

Dear guardian friends,

Kirk was recently invited to become a junior editor for *The Galactic Robotics Journal*. His job is to read articles submitted for publication for the children's section of the journal. He is to give his opinion on whether the article or not the article should be published. He found this work to be challenging until our father taught him how to write summaries.

Writing summaries helps all of us to understand and remember what we read. With our father's encouragement, Kirk has permission to get your help in writing summaries of robotics articles.

Thanks in advance for your help.

Sincerely,

*Kirk, Luke, and Ellen English*
Guardians of Grammar Galaxy

## ⭐ Step 1: On Guard & Highlight Main Points

**On Guard.** *Answer the questions or answer them verbally for your teacher.*

1. What is a profile essay?

2. What determines whether a sentence is in active or passive voice?

3. What is one benefit of writing morning pages?

4. What is parallel structure?

5. What common purpose do parentheses and the em dash share?

**Say each of these words in a sentence.** *Examples are given.*

| caliber – quality | The auto dealer only buys high-**caliber** cars. |
|---|---|
| substantial – a lot | The charity was thrilled to receive our **substantial** donation. |
| innovations – inventions | There have been many **innovations** since we bought our last computer. |

**Highlight the main points.** *Read the robotics article below. Use a highlighter to mark the main ideas. Circle any words you don't know. Write your reactions and use these annotation marks in the margins.*

| ★ | important |
|---|---|
| ♥ | favorite |
| ? | don't understand |
| ! | surprising/interesting |

### "Cyborg Facts for Kids" submitted by *Kiddle Encyclopedia*

A **cyborg** (short for "**cyb**ernetic **org**anism") is a being with both organic and biomechatronic body parts. The term was coined in 1960 by Manfred Clynes and Nathan S. Kline.

The term cyborg is not the same thing as bionic, biorobot or android; it applies to an organism that has restored function or enhanced abilities due to the integration of some artificial component or technology that relies on some sort of feedback. While cyborgs are commonly thought of as mammals, including humans, they might also conceivably be any kind of organism.

In popular culture, some cyborgs may be represented as visibly mechanical (e.g., Cyborg from DC Comics, the Cybermen in the *Doctor Who* franchise or The Borg from *Star Trek* or Darth Vader from *Star Wars*) or as almost indistinguishable from humans (e.g., the "Human" Cylons from the re-imagining of *Battlestar Galactica*, etc.).

Cyborgs in fiction often play up a human contempt for over-dependence on technology, particularly when used for war, and when used in ways that seem to threaten free will. Cyborgs are also often portrayed with physical or mental abilities far exceeding a human counterpart (military forms may have inbuilt weapons, among other things).

### Overview

According to some definitions of the term, the physical attachments humanity has with even the most basic technologies have already made them cyborgs. In a typical example, a human with an artificial cardiac pacemaker or implantable cardioverter-defibrillator would be considered a cyborg, since these devices measure voltage potentials in the body, perform signal processing, and can deliver electrical stimuli, using this synthetic feedback mechanism to keep that person alive.

### Origins

The concept of a man-machine mixture was widespread in science fiction before World War II.

The term was coined by Manfred E. Clynes and Nathan S. Kline in 1960 to refer to their conception of an enhanced human being who could survive in extraterrestrial environments:

Their concept was the outcome of thinking about the need for an intimate relationship between human and machine as the new frontier of space exploration was beginning to open up.

Cyborgs tissues structured with carbon nanotubes and plant or fungal cells have been used in artificial tissue engineering to produce new materials for mechanical and electrical uses.

**Actual cyborgization attempts**

In current prosthetic applications, the C-Leg system developed by Otto Bock HealthCare is used to replace a human leg that has been amputated because of injury or illness. The use of sensors in the artificial C-Leg aids in walking significantly by attempting to replicate the user's natural gait, as it would be prior to amputation. Prostheses like the C-Leg and the more advanced iLimb are considered by some to be the first real steps towards the next generation of real-world cyborg applications. Additionally cochlear implants and magnetic implants which provide people with a sense that they would not otherwise have had can additionally be thought of as creating cyborgs.

Since 2004, British artist Neil Harbisson, has had a cyborg antenna implanted in his head that allows him to extend his perception of colors beyond the human visual spectrum through vibrations in his skull. His antenna was included within his 2004 passport photograph which has been claimed to confirm his cyborg status. In 2012 at TEDGlobal, Harbisson explained that he started to feel cyborg when he noticed that the software and his brain had united and given him an extra sense.

Furthermore many cyborgs with multifunctional microchips injected into their hand are known to exist. With the chips they are able swipe cards, open or unlock doors, operate devices such as printers or, with some using a cryptocurrency, buy products, such as drinks, with a wave of the hand.

**In the military**

Military organizations' research has recently focused on the utilization of cyborg animals for the purposes of a supposed tactical advantage. DARPA has announced its interest in developing "cyborg insects" to transmit data from sensors implanted into the insect during the pupal stage. The insect's motion would be controlled from a Micro-Electro-Mechanical System (MEMS) and could conceivably survey an environment or detect explosives and gas. Similarly, DARPA is developing a neural implant to remotely control the movement of sharks. The shark's unique senses would then be exploited to provide data feedback in relation to enemy ship movement or underwater explosives.

The use of neural implants has recently been attempted, with success, on cockroaches. Surgically applied electrodes were put on the insect, which were remotely controlled by a human. The results, although sometimes different, basically showed that the cockroach could be controlled by the impulses it received through the electrodes. DARPA is now funding this research because of its obvious beneficial applications to the military and other areas

Eventually researchers plan to develop HI-MEMS for dragonflies, bees, rats and pigeons. For the HI-MEMS cybernetic bug to be considered a success, it must fly 100 metres (330 ft) from a starting point, guided via computer into a controlled landing within 5 metres (16 ft) of a specific end point. Once landed, the cybernetic bug must remain in place.

Mission 31: Writing Summaries

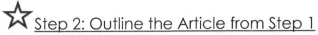 Step 2: Outline the Article from Step 1

**Write the thesis or big idea of the article.** *Then write the main points you highlighted in Step 1 into the outline below. Next, write one or two examples/explanations of each main point. Finally, write your opinion of the article. Do you think other kids would find this article interesting?* **Note:** Before outlining, look up words you circled and concepts you marked with a ?.

**"Cyborg Facts for Kids"** submitted by *Kiddle Encyclopedia*

Thesis_____

I. Main point:_____
   A. Example/explanation:_____
   B. Example/explanation:_____

II. Main point:_____
   A. Example/explanation:_____
   B. Example/explanation:_____

III. Main point:_____
   A. Example/explanation:_____
   B. Example/explanation:_____

IV. Main point:_____
   A. Example/explanation:_____
   B. Example/explanation:_____

Opinion on publication and why_____
_____

**Activity.** *With your teacher's permission, learn more about cyborgs by watching a video linked at GrammarGalaxyBooks.com/BlueStar.*

Mission 31: Writing Summaries

★ Step 3: Write a Summary of the Article in Step 1
**Using the outline you created in Step 2, type a rough draft of a one-paragraph summary.**

**Vocabulary Victory!** Do you remember what these words mean? *Check Step 1 if you need a reminder.*

| caliber | He would give his opinion on their **caliber** and whether or not they should be published. |
| --- | --- |
| substantial | It requires **substantial** reading. |
| innovations | I would be the first to know about robotics **innovations**. |

★ Advanced Guardians Only
**Edit your summary.** *Read your summary aloud. Check for spelling and grammar errors. Then ask your teacher to edit your summary. Make any changes suggested.*

**Mission 31: Update**

Dear guardians,

The editors of *The Galactic Robotics Journal* loved your summaries and opinions on whether or not articles should be published. Kirk is all caught up and is very grateful to you.

We hope you enjoyed reading the articles we sent you. Writing summaries can take time, but the results are helpful for journal editors and students alike.

We are including the solutions to your mission.

Sincerely,

*Kirk, Luke, and Ellen English*
Guardians of Grammar Galaxy

Step 1 Solutions
**On Guard.**
1. What is a profile essay? **A written description of a person, place or event.**
2. What determines whether a sentence is in active or passive voice? **If the subject of the sentence is being acted upon.**
3. What is one benefit of writing morning pages? **Creativity; better, more confident writing; improved handwriting speed**
4. What is parallel structure? **Using the same grammatical structure in a sentence.**
5. What common purpose do parentheses and the em dash share? **Enclose nonessential or extra information.**

**Highlight main points.**
Overview, Origins, Actual Cyborgization Attempts, and In the Military should be highlighted. Other annotations will vary.

Step 2 Solutions – answers will vary

Thesis   Humans are already cyborgs

Main Point I: Overview/Introduction

Main Point II: Origins/History

Main Point III: Actual Cyborgization Attempts

Main Point IV: In the Military

**Mission 32: Persuasive Speaking**

Dear guardians,

Have you heard that Parliament is considering a law that would require communicator owners to be 16 and older? We don't know how you feel about that, but we are going to try to persuade Parliament not to enact that law. Kirk is going to be speaking in front of Parliament, but we need your help.

Please write a persuasive speech that can be given to parents of kids in Grammar Girls and Guys groups, even if you agree we need a law. We want to encourage discussion before a law is passed.

Sincerely,

*Kirk, Luke, and Ellen English*
Guardians of Grammar Galaxy

Mission 32: Persuasive Speech

## ⭐ Step 1: On Guard & Research a Persuasive Speech

**On Guard.** *Highlight TRUE or FALSE for each question.*

1. Paraphrasing is a summary in your own words.  TRUE   FALSE

2. To write a profile essay, you <u>must</u> do an interview.  TRUE   FALSE

3. The passive agent is the subject of a sentence written in passive voice.  TRUE   FALSE

4. Morning pages should be edited occasionally.  TRUE   FALSE

5. This sentence is written in parallel structure: Cook enjoys baking cookies, cakes, and pastries.  TRUE   FALSE

**Say each of these words in a sentence.** *Examples are given.*

| | |
|---|---|
| **wares** – merchandise | Our neighbor brings her **wares** to sell at craft shows. |
| **thronged** – crowded | We didn't go into the store because it was **thronged** with people. |
| **thwart** – prevent | The guardians do their best to **thwart** the Gremlin's plans for chaos. |

**Research a persuasive speech.** *With your teacher's permission, do some research on children's smart phone use that will support your position. You may choose to research driving age as an alternative speech topic. Find research links at GrammarGalaxyBooks.com/BlueStar. Make a list of statistics, examples, and arguments you'd like to use in your speech on the lines below.*

Mission 32: Persuasive Speech

⭐ Step 2: Respond to Audience's Objections
**What conflicting opinions do you think your audience has on your speech topic?** *Write what your persuasive response will be to each.* **Note:** *You may need to use your research from Step 1 in your response.*

Opinion #1_____

My response:_____

_____

_____

Opinion #2_____

My response:_____

_____

_____

Opinion #3_____

My response:_____

_____

_____

**Activity.** *With your teacher's permission, watch videos with opinions on cell phone use or driving age. Find links at GrammarGalaxyBooks.com/BlueStar.*

Mission 32: Persuasive Speech

## ⭐ Step 3: Write Your Persuasive Speech Outline

**Organize your arguments by completing the outline below.** *Use keywords rather than complete sentences. You will present the three conflicting opinions and your responses you wrote in Step 2 as the reasons/responses in your outline.*

**I. Introduction**

    A. Attention-getter _____

_____

    B. Your relationship to the topic _____

_____

    C. Why it matters to the audience _____

_____

**II. Reasons People Believe** _____

    A. Reason #1 _____

        Response _____

_____

    B. Reason #2 _____

        Response _____

_____

    C. Reason #3 _____

        Response _____

_____

**III. Conclusion**

    A. Summary of arguments _____

_____

    B. Call to action _____

    C. Relate call to action to the attention-getter _____

_____

Mission 32: Persuasive Speech

**Vocabulary Victory!** Do you remember what these words mean? *Check Step 1 if you need a reminder.*

| wares | Local artists and crafters of all sorts would be displaying their **wares**. |
|---|---|
| thronged | He was grumbling as the area around the park was **thronged** with people. |
| thwart | "Dear, let's stay positive," the queen said, trying to **thwart** a fit of anger. |

Advanced Guardians Only

**Deliver your persuasive speech to parents after you've practiced and reviewed video of your talk.** *Did you change the opinion of your audience?*

**OFFICIAL GUARDIAN MAIL**

**Mission 32: Update**

Dear guardians,

    We are pleased to report that Parliament does not plan to set a legal age for owning a communicator. We know that your speeches as well as Kirk's made a difference.

    The king is pleased that so many parents told him that they were impressed with their kids' speeches. We aren't supposed to tell you this, but you can use what you learned about persuasive speaking to change your parents' minds, even if you don't give a formal speech.

    We are including the solutions to your On Guard questions.

Sincerely,

*Kirk, Luke, and Ellen English*
Guardians of Grammar Galaxy

Step 1 Solutions
**On Guard.**

1. Paraphrasing is a summary in your own words.  **TRUE** FALSE
2. To write a profile essay, you <u>must</u> do an interview.  TRUE **FALSE**
3. The passive agent is the subject of a sentence written in passive voice.  TRUE **FALSE**
4. Morning pages should be edited occasionally.  TRUE **FALSE**
5. This sentence is written in parallel structure:
   Cook enjoys baking cookies, cakes, and pastries.  **TRUE** FALSE

**Mission 33: News Articles**

Dear guardians,

You have likely heard about the robotics competition happening now. Some of you are participating in it. But you may not know that Kirk is not only participating but writing an article about it for *The Grammar Gazette*.

To prepare Kirk for writing the article, our father taught us how to write news articles and he wants us to teach you. Please complete this mission so you'll be prepared to be news reporters. You never know when you'll be needed!

Sincerely,

*Luke and Ellen English*
Guardians of Grammar Galaxy

## ★ Step 1: On Guard & Research a Competition

**On Guard.** *Highlight the correct answer for each question.*

1. The biggest obstacle to persuading an audience may be:
   not practicing     lack of interest     poor hearing

2. A multi-paragraph summary requires:
   annotation     an opinion     transition words

3. Profile essays usually involve:
   passive voice     an interview     closed questions

4. The following verb is in passive voice:
   are made     died     slept

5. Luke loves to read, to swim, and _____.
   eating     cookies     to eat


**Say each of these words in a sentence.** *Examples are given.*

| bemoaned – complained | My mom **bemoaned** leaving her wallet behind. |
|---|---|
| aura – atmosphere | The theater had an **aura** of excitement as the movie was about to start. |
| meandered – strolled | Our dog didn't run when called but **meandered** his way home. |

Mission 33: News Articles

**Research a competition.** *Decide on a competition you'd like to write a news article about. With your teacher's help, research news articles about similar competitions. Read them and note whether the articles keep your attention. Find sample news articles at GrammarGalaxyBooks.com/BlueStar.*

<u>If possible, attend the competition</u>. *If attendance isn't possible, watch news coverage of a competition. Note what you observe on the next page. Then ask a competitor, a fan, and an event organizer/announcer their views on the competition. If you are watching news coverage, include quotes from those interviewed.* **Note:** <u>Role may include team affiliation, hometown, or years of experience</u>.

**What do you notice about the venue (place) of the competition?**

**What do you notice about the audience (number, mood, attention)?**

**What do you notice about the competitors (nerves, focus, interaction)?**

**Organizer/announcer name, role, and quotes:**

**Competitor name, role, and quotes:**

**Fan name, role, and quotes:**

Mission 33: News Articles

⭐ Step 2: Outline Your News Article
**Complete the outline below, using information you collected in Step 1.**

**I. Hook to get reader interested in the competition**


**II. Basic competition information**
A. Who competed?

B. What exactly was the competition?

C. Where was the competition held?

D. When was the competition held?

E. How did the competition go?


**III. Participants' perspectives**
A. Organizer/announcer

B. Competitor

C. Fan


**IV. Summary and closure**
A. Event in summary

B. Quote, invite, or where to get more information

358

## ⭐ Step 3: Write Your News Article

**Using your outline from Step 2, type a first draft of your news article.** *Then read the article aloud and look for spelling and grammar errors.*

**Vocabulary Victory!** Do you remember what these words mean? *Check Step 1 if you need a reminder.*

| bemoaned | "You're growing up too fast!" the queen **bemoaned**. |
|---|---|
| aura | He could feel the **aura** of anticipation. |
| meandered | Kirk's anxiety became frustration as the rest of his teammates **meandered** into the arena. |

## ⭐ Advanced Guardians Only

**Have your article edited and reviewed.** Ask your teacher to mark changes that need to be made. Make the corrections to your article. Then ask someone who didn't see the competition to read your article. Did the article interest them? If it did, consider submitting the article to your local paper.

**Mission 33: Update**

Dear guardians and journalists,

    Kirk finished his news article in time for the paper's publication deadline! His teammates thought it was fun that Kirk included their quotes. The editor complimented him on adding the competitors' perspectives to what could have been a dull description.

    We loved reading your competition news articles. You did a great job making the competitions sound like fun.

    You're not in competition on this, but we are including the solutions to your On Guard questions.

Sincerely,

*Kirk, Luke, and Ellen English*
Guardians of Grammar Galaxy

Step 1 Solutions
**On Guard.**

1. The biggest obstacle to persuading an audience may be:
not practicing          lack of interest          poor hearing

2. A multi-paragraph summary requires:
annotation          an opinion          transition words

3. Profile essays usually involve:
passive voice          an interview          closed questions

4. The following verb is in passive voice:
are made          died          slept

5. Luke loves to read, to swim, and _____.
eating          cookies          to eat

**Mission 34: Compare-and-Contrast Essays**

Dear guardian friends,

You may have heard a lot about the candidates for prime minister in the upcoming election. We plan to write about the similarities and differences of the candidates in a compare-and-contrast essay for our Grammar Galaxy Kids website.

Mother says that everyone should know how to write one of these essays, so we decided to send you a mission. You can write about two political candidates for the same office or a book made into a movie. It's your choice! We look forward to reading your essays.

Sincerely,

*Kirk, Luke, and Ellen English*
Guardians of Grammar Galaxy

Mission 34: Compare-and-Contrast Essays

⭐ Step 1: On Guard & Research Your Essay

**On Guard.** *Answer the following questions or answer verbally for your teacher.*

1. What questions do news articles answer?

2. How can you connect with the audience in a persuasive speech?

3. What advantages are there to writing summaries?

4. What are two ways of organizing a profile essay?

5. Why should passive voice be used sparingly?


**Say each of these words in a sentence.** *Examples are given.*

| **outburst** – fit of temper | We all hope my little brother doesn't have an **outburst** at the store. |
|---|---|
| **intolerable** – unbearable | The heat and humidity lately have been **intolerable**. |
| **distraught** – upset | My mother was **distraught** when she couldn't find her keys. |

**Research your essay.** *After you decide on subjects to compare and contrast, make notes of similarities and differences using the Venn diagram below. If you are comparing political candidates, get your teacher's help and permission to find information. If you're comparing a book turned into a movie, read and watch both, making notes as you do.*

**Subject #1**_____    **Similarities**    **Subject #2**_____

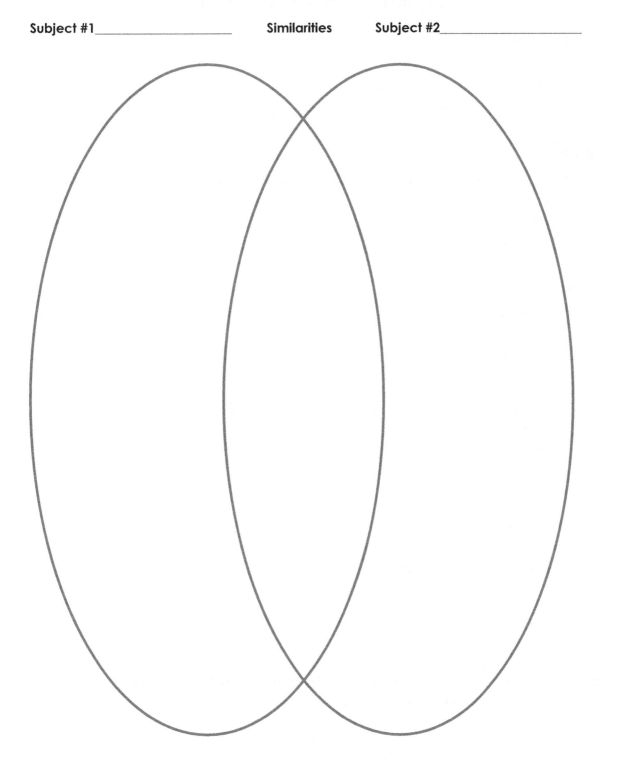

⭐ Step 2: Outline Your Essay

**Review the similarities and differences you noted in Step 1.** *Write your thesis statement for the essay. Decide if you will organize your essay by topic or by similarities and differences. Then complete the outline below.*

**I. Introduction**
    A. Attention-getter
    B. Two subjects being compared
    C. Why you're comparing them

**II. Body**
    A. Similarities or Topic #1 _____
        1. Example
        2. Example
        3. Example

    B. Differences or Topic #2 _____
        1. Example
        2. Example
        3. Example

    C. Optional Topic #3 _____
        1. Example
        2. Example
        3. Example

**III. Conclusion**
    A. Summary of similarities and differences
    B. Thesis statement/opinion _____

**Activity.** With your teacher's help and permission, find and read a compare-and-contrast essay on the same topic as yours.

Mission 34: Compare-and-Contrast Essays

## ⭐ Step 3: Writing Your Compare-and-Contrast Essay
**Using your outline from Step 2, type a first draft of your essay.**

**Vocabulary Victory!** Do you remember what these words mean? *Check Step 1 if you need a reminder.*

| outburst | He was reading the paper in the sunroom and his **outburst** disturbed the queen. |
|---|---|
| intolerable | The platform of the candidate who is running in opposition to the prime minister is **intolerable**. |
| distraught | The king was so **distraught** while watching the news that he didn't notice. |

## ⭐ Advanced Guardians Only
**Edit your essay.** *Check your essay for spelling and grammar errors. Read it aloud. Ask your teacher to edit it. Then ask your teacher or another reader what your thesis statement was. Were they correct? If not, revise your paper.*

**Mission 34: Update**

Dear guardians,

    Father was happy to hear that we were comparing Mr. Supplant with the prime minister on our website, especially because our thesis statement was that everyone should vote for the prime minister. Unfortunately, the poll numbers still show Mr. Supplant leading.

    Even so, Father wanted us to tell you that he is impressed with your compare-and-contrast essays. We found them interesting, too! We have more books and movies to add to our lists.

    Please review the solutions to the On Guard section.

Sincerely,

*Kirk, Luke, and Ellen English*
Guardians of Grammar Galaxy

### Step 1 Solutions
**On Guard.**
1. What questions do news articles answer? **The questions who, what, where, when, and how of current events.**
2. How can you connect with the audience in a persuasive speech? **Through likability, relatability, authority and by sharing why the issue matters to you and your audience.**
3. What advantages are there to writing summaries? **Helps students understand and remember important information.**
4. What are two ways of organizing a profile essay? **Chronologically and by topic.**
5. Why should passive voice be used sparingly? **It's harder to understand.**

**Mission 35: Slogans**

Dear guardians,

Have you been seeing ads for David Supplant everywhere like we have? He is doing a good job of using a slogan. His is "Focused on Our Future." We want the incumbent prime minister to have a slogan too, so we are writing one for him. We have a few ideas that we want you to review.

But we also want you to know how to write slogans yourself. Slogans are important for any form of advertising. We are including information on slogans from *The Guide to Grammar Galaxy*.

Thanks in advance for your help!

Gratefully,

*Kirk, Luke, and Ellen English*
Guardians of Grammar Galaxy

## Slogans

A slogan is a short, memorable phrase used in advertising. Slogans are used to promote the advantages of a brand, cause, or political candidate over a competitor.

**Slogans should be short.** In general, use no more than eight words.
*Just do it.* – Nike

**Slogans should be rhythmic.** Use alliteration, rhyme, or song (jingle). People remember jingles the most.
*The quilted quicker picker-upper* – Bounty
*I like Ike* – Dwight D. Eisenhower's campaign slogan
*"I'm a Big Kid Now"* – jingle for Huggies

Use slogans to truthfully (without exaggeration) communicate:
**An important benefit that sets the brand apart from the competition.**
*Nothing runs like a deer.* – John Deere
**The mission or goal.**
*We try harder.* – Avis
**Positive values and desires associated with the brand.**
*Win with Wilson* – Woodrow Wilson's campaign slogan

**Slogans are often associated with logos and taglines.** A logo is the symbol used to represent a brand. Taglines tend to be shorter and more descriptive. They are often printed with a logo.

## ⭐ Step 1: On Guard & Evaluate Slogans

**On Guard.** *Answer the following questions or answer verbally for your teacher.*

1. What are two ways of organizing a compare-and-contrast paper?

2. What should a news article begin with?

3. What is an example of an attention-getter to use in a persuasive speech?

4. What are three annotation symbols and what do they mean?

5. What is a common way of presenting information in a profile essay of a person?

**Say each of these words in a sentence.** *Examples are given.*

| **incumbent** – current | The **incumbent** mayor decided not to run for reelection. |
|---|---|
| **immensely** – greatly | Tutoring helped me with my math **immensely**. |
| **derisive** – rude | My coach said he didn't want parents making **derisive** comments during the games. |

Mission 35: Slogans

**Evaluate slogans.** *For each of our slogans for Prime Minister Gus Vanquisher, put an X in the box if we followed the rule. If you aren't sure if we followed the rule, add a ?. When you're finished, highlight your favorite slogan.*

| Slogan | Length ≤ 8 words | Rhythmic | Positive |
|---|---|---|---|
| The Gremlin is no match for Gus, so Gus is the right PM for us. | | | |
| Be sure with Gus Vanquisher | | | |
| The only man who can defeat the Gremlin | | | |
| Vocabulary, Victory, and Vanquisher | | | |
| Better a second termer than a second rater | | | |
| Some people only talk about grammar, but Gus lives it | | | |
| No more chaos because Gus has got us | | | |
| We're great with Gus! | | | |

Mission 35: Slogans

## ⭐ Step 2: Research Benefits of Brands You Love
**To practice writing slogans, first list a brand you love in each of the following categories.** Then write advantages the brand has over the competition, the mission of the company, and any positive values associated with the brand. ***Note:*** You may have to research a brand's mission with your teacher's help and permission.

**Name brand food/beverage**_____
Advantages_____
_____
Mission_____
Positive Values_____

**Restaurant**_____
Advantages_____
_____
Mission_____
Positive Values_____

**Game/toy**_____
Advantages_____
_____
Mission_____
Positive Values_____

**Attraction**_____
Advantages_____
_____
Mission_____
Positive Values_____

**Activity.** *Look for slogans this week. Which do you like and why?*

Mission 35: Slogans

☆ Step 3: Write Slogans for Your Favorite Brands

**Create new slogans for each of your favorite brands.** *Write two potential slogans for each of the brands you added in Step 2. Make sure you don't copy an existing slogan. Have your teacher or someone else choose a favorite slogan for each brand and highlight it.*

**Name brand food/beverage**_____
Slogan #1_____
_____
Slogan #2_____
_____

**Restaurant**_____
Slogan #1_____
_____
Slogan #2_____
_____

**Game/toy**_____
Slogan #1_____
_____
Slogan #2_____
_____

**Attraction**_____
Slogan #1_____
_____
Slogan #2_____
_____

**Vocabulary Victory!** Do you remember what these words mean? *Check Step 1 if you need a reminder.*

| incumbent | David Supplant was leading in the polls by a wide margin over the **incumbent** prime minister. |
|---|---|
| immensely | The guardians have improved **immensely** this year. |
| derisive | "Luke, you're being **derisive**," Ellen said. |

Mission 35: Slogans

☆ Advanced Guardians Only
**Create a new logo for one of the brands you listed in Step 3.** *Look at the company's original logo but create something different using art supplies or a graphic program.*

**Mission 35: Update**

Dear guardians,

    We are elated to tell you that the slogan you chose for Gus Vanquisher is working. He is leading in the polls and will likely win reelection. Our father couldn't be happier.

    We also want to tell you that you may have a future in advertising. Your slogans were catchy and had us wanting to eat your favorite snacks, go to your favorite restaurants, play your favorite games, and visit your favorite attractions.

    We are including the solutions to this mission.

Sincerely,

*Kirk, Luke, and Ellen English*
Guardians of Grammar Galaxy

Step 1 Solutions
**On Guard.**
1. What are two ways of organizing a compare-and-contrast paper? **By topic or by similarities/differences.**
2. What should a news article begin with? **A hook to gain the reader's interest.**
3. What is an example of an attention-getter to use in a persuasive speech? **Story, surprising statistic, humor**
4. What are three annotation symbols and what do they mean?

| | |
|---|---|
| ★ | important |
| ♥ | favorite |
| ? | don't understand |
| ! | surprising/interesting |

5. What is a common way of presenting information in a profile essay of a person? **Chronologically or by topic.**

**Evaluate slogans. – answers may vary**

| Slogan | Length ≤ 8 words | Rhythmic | Positive |
|---|---|---|---|
| The Gremlin is no match for Gus, so Gus is the right PM for us. | | X | |
| Be sure with Gus Vanquisher | X | X | X |
| The only man who can defeat the Gremlin | X | | ? |
| Vocabulary, Victory, and Vanquisher | X | X | X |
| Better a second termer than a second rater | X | X | |
| Some people only talk about grammar, but Gus lives it | | | |
| No more chaos because Gus has got us | X | X | X |
| We're great with Gus! | X | X | X |

# OFFICIAL GUARDIAN MAIL

**Mission 36: Gift Poems**

Dear guardians,

Our aunt's birthday is coming up and our mother suggested we write poems as a gift. We weren't sure what to write until Luke read more about gift poems in *The Guide to Grammar Galaxy*.

We've written our poems and we have to say it was fun. We think Aunt Iseen will love them. We aren't asking you to write a poem for her, too. Instead, we are asking you to write a poem as a gift for someone you love. We'll make the process easy for you, and we think you'll end up enjoying it like we did.

Sincerely,

*Luke, Kirk, and Ellen English*
Guardians of Grammar Galaxy

Mission 36: Gift Poems

⭐ Step 1: On Guard & Write Descriptive Words About Your Recipient

**On Guard.** *Highlight the correct answer for each question.*

1. Slogans are <u>rarely</u> used with:
   jingles      logos      more than 8 words

2. A Venn diagram is <u>most</u> likely to be used in researching:
   profile essay      news article      a compare-and-contrast essay

3. After the hook, a news article usually lists:
   basic information      quotes      where to get more information

4. A persuasive speech should include information that _____ with the audience's opinion.
   agrees      disagrees      both agrees and disagrees

5. Where is the author's opinion in a written summary usually given?
   introduction      body      conclusion

**Say each of these words in a sentence.** *Examples are given.*

| **glorious** – wonderful | Being on vacation has been **glorious**. |
|---|---|
| **jab** – insult | The comedian ignored the audience member's **jab**. |
| **inspiration** – ideas | Grandma goes to the art museum for painting **inspiration**. |

Mission 36: Gift Poems

**Write descriptive words about your recipient.** *How would you describe the subject of your poem in each of these areas? Use single words when possible.*

Personality

Work

Hobbies

Likes

Dislikes

Habits

Memories with them

Appearance (positive)

Mission 36: Gift Poems

⭐ Step 2: Find Rhyming Word Pairs

**Using a printed or online rhyming dictionary, look for words that rhyme with the words in Step 1 that would also make sense in your poem.** *For example, our aunt is <u>funny</u>. <u>Runny</u> rhymes with <u>funny,</u> and we know Aunt Iseen doesn't like her eggs runny. Write rhyming word pairs in the chart below, putting the connection in the notes section. Don't worry if you can't find rhyming words for every area in Step 1.* **Note**: <u>We put our words in the chart as an example.</u>

| Rhyming Words | Notes |
|---|---|
| funny  runny | doesn't like runny eggs |
|  |  |
|  |  |
|  |  |
|  |  |
|  |  |
|  |  |
|  |  |
|  |  |
|  |  |
|  |  |
|  |  |
|  |  |
|  |  |
|  |  |
|  |  |
|  |  |
|  |  |
|  |  |
|  |  |
|  |  |
|  |  |
|  |  |
|  |  |

**Activity.** Ask someone who knows your gift recipient for other descriptive words if you run out of ideas.

## ⭐ Step 3: Write a Gift Poem

**First, decide which poem format your gift recipient would enjoy most: acrostic, ode, sonnet, or humorous.** *We encourage you to type or write a rhyming poem. Begin by writing the first rhyming stanza. Use your rhyming word chart from Step 2. The lines may include other words from Step 1. When finished, the lines should have a similar rhythm (number of beats). Read the lines aloud. If the rhythm is off, delete or change words before the rhyming words. You may want to write the last rhyming stanza of the poem next. It will be easier to fill in stanzas to complete the poem. If you feel stuck, put the poem away for a while, or ask your teacher for ideas. Here is a humorous couplet Luke wrote for his first draft.*

***Our Aunt Iseen is pretty, sweet, and funny.***
***She loves Cook's eggs, except when they are runny.***


**Vocabulary Victory!** Do you remember what these words mean? *Check Step 1 if you need a reminder.*

| glorious | It's Aunt Iseen's birthday next week, and I have a **glorious** idea. |
|---|---|
| jab | "No, it doesn't have to be long," the queen said, ignoring Luke's **jab**. |
| inspiration | Luke went to the castle library to look through a book of poems for **inspiration**. |

## ⭐ Advanced Guardians Only

**Make the poem special.** *Put the final version in your best handwriting or a fancy font. Then frame it. Or include the poem in a photo book you present as a gift.*

# OFFICIAL GUARDIAN MAIL

**Mission 36: Update**

Dear guardian friends,

Our Aunt Iseen laughed and cried while reading our gift poems. Mother says that's the best response you can get from her sister.

We hope you had fun writing your poems and that your recipients loved them, too. We have loved doing Blue Star missions with you. What a terrific job you've done!

We are giving you the solutions to the On Guard section, and we are giving you the final challenge to complete. Review what you've learned to get 9 or more correct. Then you'll be Nova-level guardians.

Sincerely,

*Kirk, Luke, and Ellen English*
Guardians of Grammar Galaxy

Mission 36: Gift Poems

Step 1 Solutions

**On Guard.**

1. Slogans are <u>rarely</u> used with:
   jingles      logos      <mark>more than 8 words</mark>
2. A Venn diagram is <u>most</u> likely to be used in researching:
   profile essay      news article      <mark>a compare-and-contrast essay</mark>
3. After the hook, a news article usually lists:
   <mark>basic information</mark>      quotes      where to get more information
4. A persuasive speech should include information that _____ with the audience's opinion.
   agrees      disagrees      <mark>both agrees and disagrees</mark>
5. Where is the author's opinion in a written summary usually given?
   introduction      body      <mark>conclusion</mark>

# Blue Star Final Challenge I

*Carefully read all the possible answers* and then highlight the letter for the **one** best answer.

1. **Slogans should be:**
   a. short
   b. rhythmic
   c. both a and b

2. **Outlines are important in writing:**
   a. morning pages
   b. slogans
   c. essays, speeches, and news articles

3. **Kim enjoys crafts, games, and to read.**
   What is wrong with the sentence above?
   a. split infinitive
   b. lacks parallel structure
   c. passive voice

4. **She received an expensive woman's ring as a gift.**
   What is wrong with the sentence above?
   a. misplaced modifier
   b. not in progressive tense
   c. wrong grammatical mood

5. **I read because I love to learn.**
   What part of speech is the underlined group of words?
   a. adjective clause
   b. adverbial clause
   c. adverbial phrase

6. **She plays piano.**
   Which is the present perfect progressive form of the above?
   a. She will be playing piano.
   b. She has been playing piano.
   c. She will have been playing piano.

7. **Which of the following words is spelled correctly?**
   a. cheif
   b. dizeaze
   c. notice

8. **I like lessons with _____ math problems.**
   Which word belongs in the blank above?
   a. fewer
   b. less
   c. alot of

9. **Describing political leaders as children is a form of:**
   a. diminution
   b. satire
   c. both a and b

10. **Urban legends seem more believable when they include:**
    a. humor
    b. insects
    c. local details

Number Correct:_____/10

Blue Star Challenge

## ⭐ Advanced Guardian Vocabulary Challenge

For an extra challenge, highlight the word that best fits each blank.

1. **The video gave the hairdresser_____.**
   wares        inspiration        aura

2. **The bully made a _____ comment.**
   derisive        caliber        affirmation

3. **The lost child was _____.**
   thronged        substantial        distraught

4. **Customers _____ the store's closing.**
   diminished        bemoaned        subdued

5. **The guard dog tries to _____ strangers' entry.**
   thwart        influence        sacrifice

6. **People look to the tech company for _____.**
   consciousness        innovations        outburst

7. **She didn't think the story she heard was _____.**
   intolerable        legitimate        meandered

8. **Crocheting is my grandmother's favorite _____.**
   jab        incumbent        pastime

9. **News shows can be _____ for children.**
   disturbing        glorious        stay

Number Correct:_____/9

Blue Star Final Challenge 1 Answers
1.c; 2.c; 3.b; 4.a; 5.b; 6.b; 7.c; 8.a; 9.c; 10.c

**If you got 9 or more correct, congratulations!** You're now a Blue Star guardian and you are ready for the Blue Star book. See GrammarGalaxyBooks.com/shop for ordering.

**If you did not get 9 or more correct, don't worry.** You have another chance. You may want to have your teacher review the information from each chapter on the questions you missed. Then take the Yellow Star Final Challenge 2. Remember to **choose the <u>one</u> best answer**.

Advanced Guardian Vocabulary Challenge Answers
1. inspiration
2. derisive
3. distraught
4. bemoaned
5. thwart
6. innovations
7. legitimate
8. pastime
9. disturbing

# Blue Star Final Challenge 2

*Carefully read all the possible answers* and then highlight the letter for the **one** best answer.

1. **A Venn diagram is most likely to be used in writing:**
    a. morning pages
    b. a compare-and-contrast essay
    c. neither a nor b

2. **Saturn was discovered by Galileo.**
   What is true about the above sentence?
    a. It's written in passive voice.
    b. It lacks parallel structure.
    c. It would make a good slogan.

3. **Which of the following sentences uses parentheses correctly?**
    a. Exercise is shown to reduce resting heart rate (RHR).
    b. Look at my dog (she's going crazy!)!
    c. Students who read more books are better at spelling (and have bigger vocabularies, too.)

4. **Which sentence is written correctly?**
    a. My dog a German shepherd is five years old.
    b. My dog who is a German shepherd is five years old.
    c. My dog, a German shepherd, is five years old.

5. **Which sentence is written correctly in the subjunctive mood?**
    a. My wish is that all dogs be rescued.
    b. My wish is that all dogs are rescued.
    c. My wish is that all dogs is rescued.

6. **Which sentence includes a split infinitive?**
    a. He tried to carefully glue the last piece to the model.
    b. He tried to glue the last piece to the model carefully.
    c. Carefully, he tried to glue the last piece to the model.

7. **The most likely meaning of <u>thermacogenesis</u> is:**
   a. creation that uses water molecules
   b. use of a drug to increase body temperature
   c. movement of small molecules

8. **The word <u>crunch</u> is an example of:**
   a. oxymoron
   b. British vocabulary
   c. onomatopoeia

9. **Which quote of Martin Farquhar Tupper's is written correctly?**
   a. If thee art master to thyself, circumstances shall harm thou little.
   b. If thou art master to thyself, circumstances shall harm thou little.
   c. If thou art master to thyself, circumstances shall harm thee little.

10. **The primary tone of *Grammar Galaxy Blue Star* is:**
    a. serious
    b. fearful
    c. lighthearted

Number Correct:_____/10

Blue Star Challenge

## Blue Star Challenge 2 Answers
1.b; 2.a; 3.a; 4.c; 5.a; 6.a; 7.b; 8.c; 9.c; 10.c

**If you got 9 or more correct, congratulations!** You're now a Blue Star guardian and you are ready for the Nova book. See GrammarGalaxyBooks.com/shop for ordering.

**If you did not get 9 or more correct, don't worry.** Review the questions you missed with your teacher. You may want to get more practice using the resources at GrammarGalaxyBooks.com/BlueStar. Your teacher can ask you other questions like the ones you missed and if you get them correct, you'll be a Blue Star guardian, ready for the Nova book. See GrammarGalaxyBooks.com/shop for ordering.

# Official Blue Star Guardian

THIS CERTIFICATE IS TO ACKNOWLEDGE THE ACHIEVEMENTS OF

_____

ON THIS _____ DAY OF _____, 20___.

*Kirk, Luke, and Ellen English*
GUARDIANS OF GRAMMAR GALAXY

Made in the USA
Monee, IL
03 March 2024

54075876R00221